Intimate Journal
or
Here's a Manuscript

NICOLE BROSSARD

Intimate Journal
or
Here's a Manuscript

followed by

Works of Flesh
and Metonymies

Translated and with an Introduction
by Barbara Godard

THE MERCURY PRESS

The publisher gratefully acknowledges the financial assistance of the Canada
Council for the Arts, the Ontario Arts Council, and the Ontario Book
Publishing Tax Credit Program. The publisher further acknowledges the
financial support of the Government of Canada through the Department of
Canadian Heritage's Book Publishing Industry Development Program
(BPIDP) for our publishing activities.

Editor for the press: Beverley Daurio
Proofreader: Angela Rawlings
Composition and page design: Beverley Daurio
Cover design: Gordon Robertson

Printed and bound in Canada
Printed on acid-free paper
1 2 3 4 5   08 07 06 05 04

Canadian Cataloguing in Publication Data
Brossard, Nicole, 1943-
Intimate journal, or, Here's a manuscript / Nicole Brossard ; translated by
Barbara Godard.
Translation of: Journal intime, ou, Voilà donc un manuscrit.
Includes bibliographical references.
ISBN 1-55128-104-X
1. Brossard, Nicole, 1943- —Diaries. I. Godard, Barbara II. Title. III. Title:
Here's a manuscript.
PS8503.R7Z47 2004   C848'.5403   C2004-901680-6

The Mercury Press
Box 672, Station P, Toronto, Ontario Canada M5S 2Y4
www.themercurypress.ca

Introduction

The Moving Intimacy
of Language

Barbara Godard

"[L]oving you and writing stem from the same mental
function, the same desiring circuit. The same economy.
Loving you is thinking with my skin everything I am
in the unrecorded and recommencing of words."
(Nicole Brossard)

"Lightly brushing the bloom of flesh. Everything on the surface."
(Nicole Brossard)

Economies of Writing

Journaling is popularly recommended as a way to master
time's inexorable flux and consolidate a coherent self. Such
a phenomenon has the journal become in the contemporary search for self-knowledge that "journal has even
become a verb" (Baldwin 4). Temporality, writing, and the

subject are indeed Nicole Brossard's concerns in *Intimate Journal*. With a difference, however, that interrogates all representational practices with their logic of separation and substitution in the play of absence/presence of referential illusion. For, as *Intimate Journal* reflexively proclaims, it is an "optical illusion" (*JI* 27), "a fictive text that stirs up all the questions one could possibly imagine" (*JI* 61). "Can one translate what in the mind confronts the unspeakable or again what in the body confines women to the inexpressible within the symbolic field?" (*JI* 78). "Where and when does biography end?" (*JI* 33). What is the relation between words, the arc of connection? Such questions bring no certainty, but unsettle in Nicole Brossard's investigation of the "perpetual movement between living and writing" (*JI* 33), those fields of human activity so polarized by cultural conventions that accord value to the separation of art from life.

Intimate Journal challenges the binary logic of a symbolic order Brossard considers "obsolete" with a transversal movement through the space in-between, a realm where predetermined rules no longer apply. Through attention to the poetics and politics of enunciation, she has embarked on a project of making visible the dynamics of complex mediations of the in-between with their reciprocal constitution of subjects and objects. Her analysis of the networks of power and discourses that connect objects with social symbols offers a critical alternative to modernity's radical separation of mind and body, subject and object, masculine and feminine. The journal is, as she proclaims, "the shady and shadowy space of a text" in which the fuzzy image of objects forms a halo for the subject (*JI* 10). While the self writes the journal, the journal reciprocally writes the self. With a double movement in both directions out to the chaos of flows of difference and in to its own limited form, the journal creates passages between fleeting sensation and planes of consistency, between perception and form, between the visual intensity of the dazzling white light of a winter morning and the constraint of daily writing with the minimal support of "paper, pen and table" (*JI* 14). The text shuttles between lists of tasks to be undertaken (*JI* 51), allegories of its own production and reflections upon its generic ambiguity: "[m]emoir, autobiography, journal, fiction" (*JI* 48). Who distinguishes among these genres? Not *Intimate Journal*: it performatively enacts what it theorizes, writing between two discourses, between fiction and theory, never fully assuming the former while preventing the consolidation of the latter, as it creates Brossard with a difference in writing.

Through her project to create a device for conveying the smallest possible line between fiction and reality, Brossard explores how material objects and gestures in their interrelations produce utopian possibilities for transformation. Despite the "troubling violence of things," consciousness of the practice of living manifests itself "primarily in writing" (*JI* 15). Language has the power to instigate movement and events and so creates wor(l)ds of sense for a subject in the making. "The body seals and conceals a hidden language, and language forms a glorious body," such is the force of "flexion" that constitutes a "double 'transgression'—of language by the flesh and of the flesh by language" (Deleuze 280, 286). For the body is not outside or prior, but reciprocally constituted with language. In French, as Lacan reminds us, *lettre* (letter) and *l'être* (being) are homonyms: "words are embedded in all the corporeal images that captivate the subject" (Lacan 183). "Life turns on a few words" (*JI* 38), such is the moving intimacy of language that lightly touches the bloom of flesh. "Thinking with my skin," Brossard observes, articulating her corporeal logics (*JI* 65). Culture is etched on the entire surface of the skin, a screen or "surface of reading" that differs from the representational "economy of the mirror" (*DI* 97) in that texts do not reflect but produce subjects through their socio-linguistic mediation. Shattering the mirrors of representation, writing as Brossard practices engages the dynamic flow of a process that is corporeal as well as discursive. Affective bodies also work at living beyond themselves, at "sur-vival," inscribing their gestures as rhythms in the act of writing. Writing enables one to get outside the self, as Brossard "imagine[s] the sensation" it would produce to think of "writing tomorrow" (*JI* 23) when she writes the date

February 4 1983 on the entry for February 3. As it accumulates "sensation," writing becomes irrevocably intertwined with memory, creating an archive of texts and affects, one that seizes upon a moment of visceral sensation to recognize the past in its becomings. Such a parallax has the power of taking thought beyond its images of itself and the world, making it available for differentiated becomings and new forms of subjectivity.

Commissioned by Radio-Canada for a series of writers' diaries, *Intimate Journal* was written between 26 January and 28 March 1983 and broadcast over a week in August of that year. Brossard has worked with the constraints of such a format to denaturalize both writing and the construction of identity with an anti-journal which responds to the commission as to a literary challenge. Each of the five sections into which the text is divided comprised a half-hour programme read by actress Pol Pelletier. The dated entries range from a single line to several paragraphs and include notes, memories, anecdotes, reveries, aphorisms. For a long time, Brossard notes, she had "tried to cheat reality living in the virtual" of reading (*JI* 37). In addition to her reflection upon the life/writing interface, Brossard meditates on the "echographies" of radio when she plays up the dialectic in which the "live effect" and illusion of presence created by the directness of the voice contradict the temporal lag of the prerecorded material from a written script. As she wryly observes, "to think of being able to live in real time is an invention of the twentieth century" (*JI* 27). Formal constraints of the diary genre as the spontaneous "expression" of a subject are further intensified and contested with the subsequent addition to each section in the text's published version of the "postures" and poems with their repetitions and rhyme. In the seeming randomness of the repeated words in these associative series, "[w]ords... strike a pose" in that they constitute simultaneously a particular style and "a particular body" (Deleuze 286-7). Stances more than stanzas, the "postures" position themselves in the interval between word and matter. This intensification of the artifice of verbal ordering foregrounds the shift in enunciative position from voice to writing, from speaking subject to the subjectless affect of the linguistic chain. The text was further transformed by Brossard for a staged dramatic reading which, with pruning of some passages describing daily routine and the final two postures and poems, resulted in a one-and-a-half hour performance for Festival Trois in August 2003. In this dramatized version, the notion of a coherent autobiographical subject was further displaced in that the script was performed by three women. Brigitte Haentjens' direction emphasized the sonorous distinctions between three different timbres, all voicing successively what purports to be an identical "I," and so reflexively performing the slippage between word and body which Brossard's text investigates.

The formal investigation of representation as metaphoric repetition, when the words of the diary are recombined in these supplements, is subject to further interrogation in the second edition where it is juxtaposed with alternate logics of relation in the displacements of metonymic combination in "Works of Flesh." In this suite of fourteen prose poems, Brossard inverts the logic of *Intimate Journal* to begin in real time, with the body and the work of mothering, so as to explore the transmission of knowledge across generations of women who have successively given birth to each other. Nonetheless, linguistic line and blood line operate chiastically in these texts. Whereas *Intimate Journal* begins in the virtuality of reading and writing, it stutters to an end in bodily sensation. Conversely, "Works of Flesh" begins with the reunion of mother and pregnant daughter and a consideration of maternal genealogy, to end with an exchange of letters between the two women and a plea from the daughter, herself now a mother, to "write me." The exchange of linguistic signs between the two women sustains and extends their relation across time and space, and so enables the transmission of knowledge and affect between generations. This exchange between women holds out the hope of realizing Luce Irigaray's dream of an other economy of relations, one that would lead not through sublation to a transcendent subject gendered masculine, but to a sensible transversal involving interactions among embodied subjects in their reciprocal engagements with otherness within and without. The "corps-à-corps avec la mère" would result, then, neither in absorption of the one by the other through their proximity, nor to violence of the one against the other in rejection of such bodily closeness. Rather, the other would not be incorporated into the same in a logic of identification, but would relate as other to yet an other in a regime of ramifying differences.

Economies of Translation

Translation has affinities with writing, at least as Brossard understands the two practices that work with language(s) as ready-made. In a textual logic of infinite potential variation, translation indeed holds a privileged place. "The question raised in translation as in writing is that of selection," she contends: "[w]hich signifier to favour, to choose, in order to enliven on the surface the multiple signifieds that agitate invisibly at work in the depth of consciousness" (*JI* 20). Nonetheless, while writing takes the risk of thought, translating entails only pleasure in the play of language. For the writer to be translated, moreover, is to be compelled to confront the arbitrariness of her relation to language and to undergo a process of reflexive transformation in the

encounter with an other. In *Intimate Journal* Brossard introduces a metafictional inscription of translation as a disori-
enting act of rewriting. As she observes in the course of
reading the final draft of the English translation of *L'Amèr:*
"To be translated is to be interrogated not only in what one
believes oneself to be but in one's way of thinking in a language, and of being thought by the same language" (*JI* 20).
What would her relation to her body be if she "thought in
English, Italian, or some other language.... How would the
word kimono, if it had been part of my everyday life, have
modified my way of seducing and working?" (*JI* 20).
Couched here in the interrogative, the Sapir-Whorf
hypothesis that language speaks us underscores the incom-
mensurability of languages and the (im)possibility of translation in the face of its transformative powers.

Yet for Brossard this decentring in language as the self
becomes other constitutes the condition of radical possibility
for writing that challenges patriarchal hierarchies of value and
reconfigures the relation between languages, bodies and cul-
tures as malleable and multivocal processes. In her post-
Nietzschean approach to representation, rhetoric precedes
logic, word and matter are intertwined, and the plasticity of
language opens the way to endless possibilities of assemblage.
Words have the power to move us, to draw us out of ourselves. With its twenty-six letters of the alphabet, language as
combinatory constitutes a virtuality for all possible actualiza-

tions of its infinite potentiality. And it is in the "deferral of the virtual" of reading and writing that Brossard has long tried to trick (and transform) reality (*JI* 37). The temporal lag of writing is "translated" in "figures" whose rhetoricity metonymically shifts into a "relay, a transmission device," relay in which we read and where "sense figures, making an image" (*AL* 151). As reading/rewriting, translation actualizes such a virtuality, establishing a play of variation from its changed angle of perception that sets in motion a line of flight. Infolding upon itself in the doubling of translation, the text unfolds then to an outside, to the surprise of the unknown and unanticipated.

Intimate Journal not only stages the scene of translation from the perspective of the translated, but it also performs acts of translation in its self-reflexive meditation on representation as repetition with a difference. These are not the experiments in phonemic translation Brossard carries out in *L'Aviva* and *Le désert mauve,* where the repetition of sound deconstructs the relation between signifier and signified in a proliferation of homonyms. Homolinguistic translations nonetheless, Brossard's repetition of words and phrases accords primacy to selection and combination and so to the redistribution of linguistic value. Progressively abandoning the sentence as a unit of composition, she reworks the fragments from the daily entries in the "postures" and poems, juxtaposing the "attracting material" (*JI* 67) that makes relations by means of assonance and alliteration and so unsettles smooth syntactic links.

Parataxis induces a zigzag movement in which signifying surfaces overlap and refract in proliferation and dispersion. Traces of punctuation remaining in the "posture" at the end of the first section are misleading, for sentences consist sometimes only of a single verb, at others of several juxtaposed verbs. By the second such "posture," "the fuzziness of the image orders the sentence" (*JI* 38), while in the third "the rhythm of the hypothesis" has become the operative device (*JI* 52). With no punctuation or conventional grammar as directive, words may be read in many different groupings and sequences, with those alongside or those connected by sound across the page, or as "the echo of the echo" (*JI* 52) together with the first instance in an entry and/or the third instance in a poem. Signifiers even resonate across Brossard's texts and through the transforming filter of translation, as with "the proofs of *French Kiss*" (*JI* 47) which mutates into "kiss my synthesis of the real all that energy sensation speech" (*JI* 52) and shifts again into a new configuration in the poem where it reads as "my synthesis/ of the real all that sensation/ white all white" (*JI* 53). A disjunctive play of differences ensues as signifiers are repeated in new combinations not once but twice at the end of each section, this insistence displaying the arbitrariness of any ordering, subject only to the economy of desire and its politics of assemblage.

The play of repetition poses one of the greatest challenges to the translator of *Journal intime*. While in this instance "kiss" rhymes with "synthesis," just as "baise" echoes "synthèse," such is not the case with many of the pairings. A choice must be made in translating between the logic of repeated rhyme with its chance connections and the logic of meaning, of sense matched with sense. Yet even in this case, the polysemy of "baise" exceeds the English "kiss" which relates only to the prelude to and not the complete sexual act alluded to in the slang connotation of "baiser." In the "posture" and poem at the end of the first section, repetition has posed greater challenges. The selection from the entries of rhymes that compose the phrase "d'yeux n'aveugle qu'aveu" in the "posture," which is repeated as the third line in the following poem, and further modified as the final line, "m'aveu m'aveugle" (*JI* 24-25), is unrepeatable in English. Rhyme and polysemy are introduced into the English text elsewhere through the choice of "avowal" rather than "confession" for "aveu." In the poem, this creates end rhyme with "all" in the first line. As well, it introduces a new play on words that condenses a rich cluster of meanings at the heart of Brossard's text. For "avowal" is a homonym of "a vowel" and both rhyme with "arousal." As *Intimate Journal* demonstrates repeatedly, the attraction one word has for another injects the libidinal into language, sensation into intellection in an erotics of semantics.

My strategy, then, has been one of compensation, taking up the logics of relation set forth in *Journal intime* to put it to work in the different sonorities of English. At times this has led me to introduce extra words to maintain a phonemic series, as in the opening sonorous curve of the first "posture," where "dans l'oeuf l'heure à vaincre" *(JI* 24) becomes "l'oeuf love the hour to overcome," where I draw on the lexicon of tennis, "l'oeuf love," to create a slant rhyme that connects through the numerical allusion more than through assonance to time, "hour." Or again, in the "posture" and poem at the end of the third section, where "courbes brise braise de baise ma synthèse" *(JI* 52) is rendered as "curves breach braise of kiss my synthesis" culminating in the poem as "curve break braise my synthesis." Here the literal sense of "braise" as "embers" is diminished in English where "braise" refers to a way of cooking rather than to live coals. Both, however, connote heat and hence emotional intensity. In the same section, while it is possible to retain the repetition of "vacille oscille" *(JI* 52) in "vacillate oscillate," the third instance of the rhyme "cils" vanishes in the English "eye-lash." The play on "i" as "eye," however, performatively enacts the problematics of the porous subject that is a major preoccupation of Brossard in *Intimate Journal*. For the play of repetition is most insistent where it makes connections between heterogeneous strands central to the text's meaning. Or perhaps this should be rephrased to point out that, on the contrary, it is the very fact of repetition and its intensive engagement that makes these webs significant. The power of the pen to produce the effect of the real is underscored in the parallelism of verticality that links pen to tower, a "pen that I keep vertical" with the "sensation of vertigo" experienced at the top of the Tokyo Tower (*JI* 21), parallelism conveyed through the repetition of the phonemes in "vertical" and "vertigo" which, in the phonic economy of the French language, leads to "vers," meaning both "towards" and "verse." "Fervent relays" (*NV* 13), these sonorous connections with their unanticipated conjunctures reach beyond meaning, clearing a space for the emergence of new images of thought.

The relays of English transmit sense differently, accentuating the creative wandering of Brossard's compositional process to make images diverge. Translating a text that already stages its own translation, the translator is caught in the tension between language's possibility of initiating change as well as of maintaining continuity in dominant systems. In the play of heteroglossia, the translator assists at the carnival of languages or, more precisely, at the wake—Joyce's wake. *Finnegans Wake* is one of many allusions in Brossard's intertextual play with the fragment. The temptation it holds out of macaronic translation weighs in the balance against the ethical constraint of "fidelity" to *two* languages. Tracking down the numerous quotations was a significant challenge in the translation process. Translating, like writing, is research, though this kind of search to locate and fix the known is antithetical to Brossard's emphasis on experiment with the open-ended space of textual becoming, what she calls, after Claude Gauvreau, "explorean" (*JI* 45). Yet once located, the quotes amplified the Joycean polyvocality and multilingualism. *Ulysses*, according to her quote from Joyce, is "eighteen books in eighteen languages" (*JI* 23). Not only did each intertextual strand increase the complex layering of what seemed on the surface a relatively straightforward text, refracting and so multiplying its meanings, but, when identified, the quotations proved to have been worked upon in the shuttling between languages just as much as the linguistic matter itself. Indeed, one of the quotes from *Finnegans Wake* was expanded in the French version through play on the sounds (*JI* 17), appropriately, in view of Joyce's text that celebrates the generative powers of language triumphing over the death of the body and the omnipotence of author or reader. As *The Book of the Dead* reminds us, Thoth was not only the inventor of the hieroglyph and writing, but his power was such that he was able to bring Osiris back from the dead, his power to create the world by the sound of his voice alone, working also through the magic of writing to resurrect and recreate what has become deadened or clichéd.

Brossard has entered into this spirit of transforming such ready-mades, reworking even the quotes, as she does with the opening lines of celebrated *nouveaux romans* by Camus, Aquin and Ducharme that begin with the death of the mother or being devoured by objects in which she transforms the incipit of "Today" into a litany of "Yesterdays," consigning these fictions to the past (*JI* 48). The Joycean carnival of languages manifests itself also in her introduction of portmanteau words such as "ocommencer" (*JI* 24) and "rexte" (*JI* 24) and in the mingling of words in several languages in the text. Adopting these principles, I have reworked such terms as "obegin," with its paradoxical linking of end and origin, and introduced neologisms such as "recommencement" (*JI* 35) according to the same logic of contradiction, but also to retain the repetition of "re" in a phrase about the "unrecorded and recommencing of words" (*JI* 65) as well as the insistence on the syllable "re" and the dynamic principle of repetition—less visible in "beginning again." Repetition in a new context is also the way she alludes briefly to her own early writing, traces active in the textual web in phrases such as "lovhers" (*JI* 35) and "(Mother)sea" (*JI* 101). However, proverbs, another type of ready-made, albeit somewhat clichéd, proved more resistant to translation since they are so language bound. Nonetheless, at least one proverb, which at first seemed untranslatable, led ultimately to a complex reworking that multiplied rather than reduced the potential meaning of the passage when I translated the proverb, "une femme avertie en vaut deux" (*JI* 101), both literally as "a feminist is worth two women" and for the sense as "forewarned is forearmed." This enabled me to tease out both networks of value and of knowledge in respect to gender that Brossard introduces in this section in the very "zigzagging" approach to meaning-making she favours (*JI* 101). In the spirit of the pluralingualism of Brossard's text, I have retained words in foreign languages, underlining terms that appeared in English in *Journal intime* so as to add to the polyglossia visually through graphic play. I have also inserted words in French such as the couplet "ferai, fera" that contribute to a sonorous chain including "ferry" and "fairy" (*JI* 41). And I invented a few words of my own, turning "ruse" (*JI* 37) into a verb to create parallels with "muse" (*JI* 52), terms used by Brossard in relation to a discourse of the unreal. In most cases, after locating Brossard's quotations, I chose to back translate into English, rather than to cite the original, and so emphasize their performative over pedagogic function. Keeping to this spirit, I have not identified them in the body of the text, but listed the relevant texts among the references at the end for reasons of copyright. The expanding web of fragments participates thus in an infinite process of becoming rather than fixing meaning or identity in either telos or origin.

The fiction of the subject is Brossard's central concern in the journal, but this is a subject produced as an effect of writing. The subject emerges in the place of language where "I" is only a convenient term for somebody who has no real being—a shifter or relay. A "self-portrait" is created through the eyes of the self as other, as sentence fragments and predicateless statements are multiplied, giving greater weight to objects. This decentred portrait is part of a general process of flattening in the journal in which the figure is scattered over what has traditionally been negative space, so blurring the distinction between foreground and background, between subject and object. Brossard's challenge to this dualism which also encompasses the separation of mind and body takes the form of an active mixing of contradictory orders in a relation of implication, a mixing materialized at the textual surface in the device of the middle voice. Voice is the linguistic category involving relations between the subject and a process. Whereas the "active voice denotes a process that is accomplished outside the subject" in a relation with an object, "the middle voice indicates a process centering on the subject who is inside the process" as object of which s/he is an agent (Benveniste 148). The middle voice may be expressed in the French language in a number of different ways, through certain nominal forms of the verb such as infinitives, and especially through reflexive verbs and the pronoun "on" which may be either personal or impersonal, both active and passive. English does not have as rich a repertoire of devices for the middle voice, relying on the nominal verbal form of the participle to convey an action being performed on oneself. Consequently, translating the middle voice into English is inevitably a challenge, one that I have tried to meet here with the relatively unusual resources of the infinitive and the pronoun "one," introduced as a tactic of making strange to draw attention to Brossard's play with the virtual and thinning of the subject.

Everything is "material for sensations" (*JI* 62) with the power to captivate and disturb and so precipitate the spiral of "intense moments of existence" (*JI* 64). Things make one "levitate above everything" (*JI* 64), turn the world upside down or seduce one out of one's language into another order of existence, as does a silk kimono brushing softly against the body (*JI* 20). Intimacy is such a sudden "enthusiasm," an "arresting moment when life decides without it being possible to add a word" (*JI* 15), lifting one out of the self in a moment of pure ecstasy: "in ecstasy a fluid body coming from the everyday to reach the limit of voices" (*JI* 68), to reach the limit of language. For Brossard, such dispersion and potentiality release creative energy that ramifies in becoming-other.

What begins to emerge in *Intimate Journal* is the Nicole Brossard who will appear in *Baroque d'aube* as an English speaking novelist. Through the play of doubling and repetition, she comes into view in the following pages in the baroque refractions of my translation.

Works Cited

Aquin, Hubert. 1967. *Prochain épisode*. (1965). Trans. Penny Williams. Toronto: McClelland and Stewart.

Baldwin, Christina. 1991. *One to One: Self-Understanding through Journal Writing*. New York: M. Evans & Co.

Benveniste, Emile. 1971. *Problems in General Linguistics*. Trans. Mary Elizabeth Meek. Coral Gables: University of Florida Press.

Brossard, Nicole. 1988. *Aerial Letter*. (1985). Trans. Marlene Wildman. Toronto: Women's Press.

_____. 1997. *Baroque at Dawn*. (1995). Trans. Patricia Claxton. Toronto: McClelland and Stewart.

_____. 1984. *Double impression*. Montreal: Les éditions de l'Hexagone.

_____. 1998. *Journal intime* suivi de *Oeuvre de chair et Métonymies*. 2nd ed. rev. Montreal: Les Herbes rouges. *Intimate Journal or Here's a Manuscript* followed by *Works of Flesh and Metonymies*. Trans. Barbara Godard. Toronto: Mercury, 2004.

_____. 1992. *La Nuit verte du parc labyrinthe*. Montreal: Trois.

Camus, Albert. 1988. *The Stranger*. (1942). Trans. Matthew Ward. New York: Knopf.

Deleuze, Gilles. 1990. *The Logic of Sense*. (1969). Trans. Mark Lester with Charles Stivale. Ed. Constantin V. Boundas. New York: Columbia.

Ducharme, Réjean. 1966. *L'avalée des avalés*. Paris: Gallimard. *The Swallower Swallowed*. Trans. Barbara Bray. London: Hamish Hamilton, 1968.

Godard, Barbara. 2004. "Writing Machine for Changing the Subject: Nicole Brossard's *Journal intime*." in *Nicole Brossard: Essays on Her Works*. ed. Louise Forsyth. Toronto: Guernica.

Irigaray, Luce. 1985. *This Sex Which Is Not One*. (1975). Trans. Catherine Porter. Ithaca: Cornell.

_____. 1981. *Le corps-à-corps avec la mère*. Montreal: Les Éditions de la Pleine Lune.

Lacan, Jacques. 1966. *Écrits I*. Paris: Seuil.

Intimate Journal
or
Here's a Manuscript

Unless it serves as annal or historical record, the journal seems to me a place where the subject turns around and around to the point of exhaustion. In the void, the subject is sidelined from action.

In the contemporary West, the subject emerges tautological and can have no meaning, that is to say, an imaged and imaginary influence, unless cast back into a terrifying/ecstatic world that will not be a binary one, however. The subject survives three-dimensional and loses an excessive amount of time in despair, boring itself to death with nostalgia in the face of the plural mourning it must perform for an obsolete symbolic order. In a decadent patriarchal binary setting, the subject lives surrounded by characters and by nobody. The subject lives in the congestion of signifiers. Hypertrophied with emotions, the subject annuls itself in emotion. The subject no longer resists the progaganda of the subject. It is everywhere at once: in manuscript, in photocopy, in book, in note, it blinks at the end of the line on the cathode screen. The subject is conscious of everything about which it does not yet have an *idea*. Immobilized in its synthesis of itself, the subject is nonetheless at the height of its powers of discernment, attentive, the word on the tip of the tongue; but all you see is the slow movement of the mouth that suffers from the void, like a comparison really and only in comparison.

The journal is the shady and shadowy space of a text. A grey zone with no real equivalent. If reality is invented on paper by intervening in language, it is futile, nevertheless, to exacerbate the subject. Of course, one only has one life and there are so many others. One signs the other lives: the life of thought, of consciousness, the only lives apt to translate our experience of reality. If consciousness of self accompanies the sense of the real that occupies us, what preoccupies us, that is to say the anecdote, is an encumbrance just when you think you're dealing with the self. To cry over the self is to "cry over nothing." To laugh about the self is to laugh for nothing. So it is *as if egoless* that I can write, that I can be with certainty.

At the end of each of the passages that composed a programme for broadcast, I felt it necessary to add what I call a "posture," a gesture of a text, and a poem. Undoubtedly so that *nothing* escapes me and that everything can begin.

"I know: to keep a journal, you must have nothing to do,
so nothing to write."

Jean-Paul Sartre

"It's a proof of civilization to be able to contemplate suffering
from a distance."

Virginia Woolf

"Confess the unconfessable: abolish the unavowable: the journal."

Alix Cléo Roubaud

1

26 January 1983

It is twenty-four past nine, and sitting at my work table, I am trying to avoid the everyday, the abiding continuity that comes to an end only at the moment one can no longer adequately name it reality. Around me, everything resembles what I imagine and I try to imagine myself as concretely as possible. As real as possible my life that is only a tissue of words. Let it be understood, nevertheless, that I don't like to make much of my life, even between the lines.

Today, I reread a few pages of what others would call "my diary." But I have never kept an intimate journal. At most, three black notebooks in which once or twice a year I inscribe something that enables me to verify that I still exist. From one year to the next, the text varies little. Generally, I note "I'm suffering," just that and nothing more, and I close the notebook again. Sometimes it happens that I write: I exist. To have to write "I exist" is proof enough for me in a time of crisis. It's the least of things not to have to provide proof of one's existence every day. It's the minimum even though I know millions of women who are obliged to prove it every day. Some cry out, others grimace, others split their sides laughing, others rub their hands as though to spark flames, others think that an existence filled with words is like a black hole in the cosmos; still others say that to exist is to speak through matter, or again that to exist is to trace a path with one's mouth and breath in the infinite beginnings of matter.

Ten o'clock and twenty-one seconds

Each instant is important for what the mere fact of thinking about the instant arouses in me. If life is made up of precious moments, one can't say the same for the daily routine that swallows us up minute after minute in another twenty-four hours useless to resist. So, from one moment to another, I am in the process of inventing myself like this morning, sunny, glacial, white before noon. Blinding. White. Terribly white. It's the weather: it's white and bright. At the moment, everything vibrates. The light fills the entire space, infiltrates the morning, silently seeping, soaking in, and it is as though I suddenly saw everything in detail. The whole room I'm in is invaded by a thousand structures that fill up the space, that empty the space, leaving the familiar objects without any shadow. In this room, moreover, there is only the indispensable: paper, pen, table, and me. Not even a dictionary, not a single ruler. And the frost blinds me, it's the frost; don't ask me what my life will be, don't ask me what it has been. I won't tell anything. The journal is blinding me. What a strange morning for someone who likes to write.

Ten fifty

What can one say in a journal that one couldn't say elsewhere? What memory do we address when we claim to bring the past to life again, however near the past might be? What is so intimate about a journal that it could not be shared, opened by someone else's reading? Intimate. The Japanese have an expression, *mono no aware*, that signifies the "moving intimacy of things." That, I believe, is what in my life borders on the troubling violence of things. Volcano. Such dimensions foster the intuition of an existential practice whose consciousness displays itself primarily through writing. If writing is lucidity, it remains nonetheless the support for a display; displaying a life as one posts a sign in a social and political context. Pinned to the wall of the culture of my life. My text. Nothing less than that so as to learn how to read. And then, what is intimacy if not enthusiasm, a profound inspiration of the being who, as if suddenly rendered breathless, searches for its source. This arresting moment when life decides without it being possible to add a word.

Noon, 26 January 1983

Noon, white, light on reality. The everyday cuts into reality. Julie is sitting in the living room reading *How Wang-Fô Was Saved* by Marguerite Yourcenar. Well-behaved like an image, as if the flu and the teachers' strike stimulated in her feverish eyes a taste, a thirst for reading. I think of the daughter of HD who, in her preface to *HERmione*, relates the daily life of a mother who thinks only about writing, shutting herself up in her office for hours at a time. There were long silences, effect of fear, followed by the tapping of typewriter keys. It was always: "Hush, hush... 'your mother is working.'" And Frances Perdita Aldington went on to say how her two mothers, Hilda and Bryher, were in fact to their Victorian society: Mrs. Richard Aldington and Mrs. Robert McAlmon. Yes, the everyday cuts into reality. The daily life of lesbian couples. All those couples who entered Natalie

Barney's salon, at 20 rue Jacob, the fascinating couples Gertrude Stein and Alice B. Toklas, Sylvia Beach and Adrienne Monnier, Radcliffe Hall and Una Troubridge. Artist couples. As though couples of women were couples of artists. As though creation were an inevitable staging of this cast of mind in which a woman projects her entire being onto another woman the best of herself who, like an auspicious intelligence in the imaginary, gives her the energy to conceive.

28 January 1983

It's obvious that keeping a journal is like keeping house. You have to get used to the idea!

30 January 1983

The opening of Francine Simonin's exhibition of drawings, watercolours, and engravings. I walked for a long time, slowly along Saint-Denis, sad like a Sunday the day after the night before. I like walking in my city. I like everything I see there because it compels me to see. And on Saint-Denis, I see simultaneously and alternately three generations, four sexes, numbers even and odd who are going here into a café, there into a church, across from the tobacco shop, beside the sauna.

At the Gallery Treize on Duluth, there are the *Tribal Feasts,* the *Tribades,* and the beautiful series of *Homages to Maria Callas.* I walk from one piece to another, attentive and alert before Francine's work. Then, at the Gallery Aubes, I look again and again at *Madone des Sleepings* and several times at *Madone des Sleepings* in watercolour and I say to myself that it must certainly have some relation to my reading last night. Yes, it all comes back to me: "Rain. When we sleep. Drops. Drain. Sdops. But wait until our madonna of sleepings passes. Who will dry our tears."

On the way back, Jeanne Mance park viewed from the bus comes just to eye-level like a grey winter sequence, then I slowly make my way forward toward the vacant lots in Pasolini's *Mama Roma.* Entering the image and the season, at eye-level, I catch myself by surprise imagining an art of living that can contain all the nostalgia one knows oneself capable of and on which a certain taste for art depends.

Rome, 15 March 1981

From my room, I hear the music announcing the protest in preparation, Piazza Navona, against illegal abortion. The demo is being organized by the Communist Party. Women are few and far between, Piazza Navona, the click of high heels on the stone. Bar Navona.

Piazza Navona, Santa Agnese church. Marble, candles, microphones, mass. Piazza Navona, a woman sings, imploring. The microphone echoes her.

At the hotel, a doorman stands at the entrance, hands behind his back; he is looking, head turned a bit toward the left, at a young blond man. At the registration desk, sensations are lively. At the cash, a man leans on the numbers.

Piazza Navona, leaving the hotel, a woman slowly ties her scarf around her neck. It is cold in radiant Rome. Piazza Navona, I buy a collection of Pasolini's poems: *Poesia in forma di rosa.*

Rome, 31 July 1963

A night so clear. A marvellous moon. Sonia, Dante and Vincente. We walk as far as the Coliseum. It's fabulous, Rome by night. For a moment, I thought I was one of Fellini's characters. But that didn't last very long and I spoiled the night a bit by wondering whether a Fellinian character in my head was female or male. Later during the day of August 1st 1963, we walked along the Via Appia. We stopped in a little bar and we laughed and drank. But what is the laughter of a girl of twenty?

2 February 1983

I received your postcard my love and I read it again and again. It's crazy how much I depend on every word you write. From the most banal remark to the slightest ellipsis, each letter traced by you justifies my fetishism of the post card. And then, there are the words that make me tremble. Today, I know that time is going to organize itself around what I read by you, what I see of you in this handwriting. And your signature, an initial, indecipherable for someone who doesn't know it. Since our first meeting, I haven't exhausted any of the images I have of you. Each one is intact, integral, indivisible. Undoubtedly it's what they call amorous tension. A tension that empties of their meaning the words one might pronounce. I know, in these moments, that none of them could really signify. Words then become forms in mental space. They are like signs tracing the very structure of the tension. Those are the words that interest me, words which, isolated or grouped, make sense only in the ephemeral form I glimpse. I'm not speaking here about linguistic structure, I'm speaking about the form of energy I fantasize by drawing on two categories: words and thought.

3 February 1983

I devoted the whole day to reading the English translation of
L'Amèr whose final draft Barbara Godard has just sent me.
Exhausting work it is to read a text of one's own in translation. Tiring, because to the mental operations one performs in
writing the text is added the process I shall call unveiling.
Because what one chooses to hide in a text must now be
exposed. Where criticism, for example, can only presume,
dream or imagine a meaning, translation seeks to ascertain. In
this process of corroboration, I must confront what I have
consciously and scrupulously hidden from myself. To be translated is to be interrogated not only in what one believes oneself to be but in one's way of thinking in a language, and of
being thought by the same language. It means I have to question myself about the other I might be if I thought in English,
Italian, or some other language. What law, what ethics, what
landscape, what picture would then come to mind? And who
would I be in each of these languages? What would feminin-
ity have reserved for me in Italian? What relation would I have
had to my body if I had had to think it in English? How
would the word kimono, if it had been part of my everyday
life, have modified my way of seducing and working? The
question raised in translation as in writing is that of selection.
Which signifier to favour, to choose, in order to enliven on

the surface the multiple signifieds that agitate invisibly at work in the depth of consciousness? Formally is how I must compensate, so the energy that nourishes my thought does not turn against me, so that language itself does not turn against the woman I am.

How would the word kimono, if it had been part of my everyday...

Tokyo, 17 May 1982

A shadow is an undecidable theme from the height of the Tokyo Tower. From the top of the Tokyo Tower, dressed in black school uniforms, the girls are thinking about a big kimono restraining them. But the abyss, the abyss.

This morning, I walked in the streets of Tokyo. Quite a long time despite the early hour when the streets are still empty. At five a.m., I am looking for a place to drink a cup of coffee and write. In the Roponggi district, I found a Dunkin Donuts and I know despite the international appearance of the counter that I am well and truly in Japan. In spite of "You were on my mind" and "I had a dream" playing endlessly. I am in Tokyo between reality and fiction. I am emptied of all passion. I am a sea of silence between past and present. I am a geisha sitting in front of a computer, holding a honey doughnut in my left hand and in my right a pen that I keep vertical so as to trace in a few signs the sensation of vertigo I experienced yesterday morning at the top of Tokyo Tower.

Kyoto, 27 May 1982

The Golden Pavillion gleams in the pool like Mishima's breast. I must pull myself together. S. takes me by the arm and we make our way forward with great concentration among the little paths that line the ground around the Pavillion.

Kyoto, 28 May 1982

I know that I'll soon be without words to speak. I am oscillating between the sacred and the profane like a monk counting his money. Each temple moves me, each garden. Never have so many suicides been counted in literature. However, it's by millions that smiles must be spoken about here. There's an uncanniness that goes straight to the cortex. One doesn't need to talk about signs here. It's quite simply a mark of the attention I am giving to the softness of silk when I happen to brush against a woman passing by in a kimono.

Kyoto, 29 May 1982

On waking, I saw your shoulder and instantly the rice-paper door; between the two, the trees in the garden. In the corridor, I hear the padded footsteps of someone approaching. The tatami shifted during our sleep. You open your eyes. Tea is served. We drink it slowly. Each mouthful is a vision of Ryoan-ji.

4 February 1983

I shifted the date of my journal by one day so as to imagine the sensation it would give me to think that I am writing tomorrow. Yesterday, I waited desperately for a letter, a post card that never arrived. Today, I began to read the translation of *Finnegans Wake*. I stopped at page seventy-four: "But wait for the madonna of sleepings to pass. Who'll dry our tears. Sdops." During the day, I also read what Joyce said about *Ulysses*: "I 've written 18 books in 18 languages."

It's heart-breakingly cold. I am investigating the fragment. Fragment of sensations, of life, of a work. I examine myself inside and I discover nothing that can hold my attention for the moment. I prefer to leave myself until later.

It's a beautiful day. It's none of my doing. I'm examining the fragment and what must be understood by the expression: a day in the life of Nicole Brossard.

l'oeuf love the hour to overcome and sitting at a table in a way too valiant i am trying to avoid everydayness to levitate at a pleasurable moment come adequate to name reality around me emotion assemble all that imagines mimes concretely possible also my life is born weaves smooth word that is not heard life between the lines by day gleams of daylight read several more pages from the journal o at the very most see black notebooks because yesterday in the year something exists still in body o really outdated setting proves cries in time of crisis: enough. Trace fills the mouth to infinity obegin matter. Rext here second eyes blinded only by avowal: structure ruptures pass to the object of desire. Filter details. Tilt. Insist on wanting to resist avowal blinds me. Vitalife decides forms mixes mother imaginary: a couple. Thirteen tribades at dawn these lesbians pass at eye-level. i thought cruel snag read the night Fellini these are words barely translated kimono silk modifies the body of the schoolgirl you write vertical gleams by day in the pool in literature there are millions possible a single day later nothing still more writing your name

around emotion assemble all
by day gleams of daylight
eyes blinded only by avowal
at night there are some words
i avow blind me

2

24 February 1983

Tonight, I'm writing my journal but I don't understand yet what's at stake in the subject. Does one write a journal, as if, as they say, I'm going to tell everything? Is that enough? And why should it be? Certainly, the world begins with us. It's an optical illusion, of course, but one of a certain dimension, not quite enough for history, yet the only one with which we can think about remaking the world and taking stock of our existence; measuring the fullness of our desires.

To think of being able to live in real time is the only illusion in which I find the courage and pleasure of writing. Because all life of the mind is articulated in delayed time no matter whether the differential is calculated in micro-seconds or in light-years. To think of being able to live in real time is an invention of the twentieth century, a kind of "new novel" with strong sensations that leaves me suspended in the sounds of the fury of writing.

Normandy, Cerisy-la-Salle, August 1980

I'm sitting in the room in the chateau where the working sessions on the decade of Quebec literature take place. A young woman is sitting beside me; another resembles Isak Dinesen, the Danish novelist, as she appears as a pierrot and ravishing woman on a postcard. I look from one to the other, I write in my notebook that they make me dream, in a parallel entry I note a quotation from Flaubert, I am listening to a theorist at the same time as I watch the clouds pass over, clouds that form as I watch, announcing the storm, wet grass, dampness, insomnia.

Cerisy, pinnacle of theoretical debates, Cerisy Ricardou, Sarraute, Butor, Robbe-Grillet, Cerisy the Nouveau Roman. Yes. But above all, Cerisy is an atmosphere. Bats at nightfall, petanque, ping-pong, evenings of rock and roll and Calvados. Cerisy, it's theoretical and enchanting like the slogans on our North American T-shirts. California Mickey Mouse, Marilyn and Deep Purple in the heart of Normandy for a new narrative.

Cerisy's the old new novel that comes to life with theory at nine a.m. like a new narrative after coffee. There are long walks, snatches of conversation, specialists, people who bond in friendship, their desires, their topics. A bit of literature takes responsibility for a bit of sociology, some linguistics, a little psychoanalysis, in a great many words, what seduces in delayed transmission.

Cerisy, 13 August 1980

I'm sitting in the garden. Beside me, a red-headed poet with a secular imagination is looking at the landscape. We have our ballpoint pens and notebooks within easy reach. We converse unhurriedly, outlining in our heads, he, science-fiction characters, I, what could become a novel. Two women, one a redhead, are busy picking up the coffee cups the invited participants have left scattered here and there on the tables. We smoke slowly. We speak slowly. In the distance a Quebec writer is jogging; Louisa and Oriana Spaziani are making their way toward the village. Someone is playing the piano; it must be the German who never speaks. Roger Des Roches and I are talking about France as if about a book we will have read a long, long time ago, a book filled with cigarette butts, cafés, chateaux, perfumes, and writing. We are talking in the pure silence of the afternoon, but basically... in the depths of this silence, we think only about writing.

Paris, 19 August 1980

A sleepless night. And yet, I'm alive. In that case, then!

Montreal, 28 February 1983

Thinking about remaking the world or imagining it. I examine this actual experience in real time as practised in conversation, smile, tears, or laughter.

The same day

How to confront the essential? What is the quintessential? It's always abstract, wordless, and yet it's a word, an image, a mental perspective. The brain keeps surprises in store for us. These are the only things that matter to me. Surprises and riddles to decode.

3 March 1983
En route to Victoria, British Columbia

For two days I haven't stopped writing. I hadn't foreseen anything. Inspired, as they say. Now, I'm catching my breath. But
which one? First, I'll read Charlotte Perkins Gilman's *The
Yellow Wallpaper*. A beautiful agonizing text. Then, I'll open, I
open Clarice Lispector's *The Stream of Life*. It takes my breath
away. Radiance, beauty, intensity. I read no more than two or
three lines at a time. I am almost trembling. I'm excited,
incredulous, before such beauty.

Vancouver. From the airport, I head downtown in order to
get the hydrofoil that will take me to Victoria. The taxi driver talks to me about the Bible, about the parallelism of languages, he says that women poets think about their careers
instead of thinking about their duty as mothers. He's mad like
an image of a cradle cast into a raging sea. He's more danger-
ous than a Jesuit converted to pornography. The taxi driver is
so nice, so pleasant, that you no longer see the lamb he is
patiently strangling.

Victoria, later the same day

In the small port of Victoria it's spring. Such a beautiful light, the smell of the sea. I say beauty, beauty, a bit like Pol Pelletier in *A Clash of Symbols*. Yes, beauty, and I sink into the greatest sense of well-being, solicited by the clemency of the climate. My good humour is boundless. Lauri, with whom I am to stay for the weekend, comes to meet me. We take a taxi. The driver's a poet, too! Another who knows everything. Then he asks us if we know the poet Pat... Lauri immediately replies yes and this woman was murdered by her husband. "My uncle was a bastard," said the driver and nobody thought of adding anything at all.

Victoria, 4 March 1983

I am here to participate in a poetry festival. Fifteen women will read their work during the three sessions of readings that have been planned. In the morning, I walk for a long time on the streets of the little town of Oak Bay. The perfume of the cherry trees in bloom accompanies me right to the sea. Beauty, beauty. Then my head fills with the names of trees and ferns: Licorice Fern, Forsythia, Prunus Cerasifera, Arbutus. Arbutus Street, Lauri will say, is the most beautiful street. For a brief moment, I thought of the *Route de la Trace* in Martinique, but I know there is really no relation.

Then it's the first meeting with the poets. Beauty, beauty of faces, the proud bearing of bodies, the tenacity of their gazes, an English sense of humour. I relive the same emotion I knew at the time of *A Clash of Symbols* and *Têtes de pioches.* They are all <u>wonderful</u> these women from the Prairies, mountains, and Upper Canada. Some of them recount terrible things in their poems, and others are terribly funny in the moment of truth of their half-hour reading. I listen to their voices. They pronounce the names of landscapes by the seaside, in the mountains, and they also speak about what happens in the living rooms of the <u>middle</u> <u>class</u> or in shacks lost in the backwoods. Later in the evening, when we are partying, they remember Ireland, or Scotland, or Poland, and their eyes light up in a different way as if to make a country young again. And later still in the evening, the country is rejuvenated and transformed into an Indian woman sitting in a village of Cowichan or Bella Coola and the country becomes a ritual of vivid colours. Then the country ages again and the Indian woman is waiting on the streets of Vancouver while a white client approaches her, saying, "<u>How much</u>?" and, like the salmon reascending the river, she knows when climbing the stairs what awaits her.

Night of 5 March 1983

Sleepless night because I have to take an airplane very early in the morning and I prefer not to sleep. Conversations. Some tea. More tea. We exchange books. Now it's time to leave for the airport. We take the road that hugs the coast. Dawn, the sea, arbutus trees, big cedars. Fatigue stretches the gaze. I no longer know whether it's the Orient or Canada in the distance. On my return, <u>Montreal seems a strange city</u>. Taxi!

7 March 1983

There's perpetual movement between living and writing. Really, it may be between writing and writing. Private life, writing life. "She lived on words," they'll say one day. So what's the use of a journal, then? In the last few days, I realize I'm more attentive to what I'm doing, to the appointments I make, to the people I meet, to the events in which I participate, as if it were a matter of ensuring the continuity of this journal. I find that perverse. The subject is getting sucked in.

Is the life of an author a private life? Where and when does biography end? Perhaps biography is only what surrounds the writing subject, a sort of blurred halo resembling childhood or death.

Le Carbet, Martinique, 1 November 1981

Six o'clock and night already. The rustle of insects. S. is writing a postcard. Michèle is resting while I read the text of her interview with Djuna Barnes. Adrenalin writing. Martine, whom we call Martin, is analyzing the results of ultrasounds she has brought back from the hospital. She says that tomorrow she will give me an ultrasound. An echo. My heart laid bare. I say that the graphics are so beautiful I want one for a book cover. Lives, trajectories, hallucinations. Later, we are going to Saint-Pierre the village that was forcibly reborn from its ashes one day. It's All Saints Day and the cemetery is lit with candles. We walk among the graves. Dressed in their most beautiful dresses and their best suits, women and men chat beside their dead. A little farther, on the church steps, a young nun prays fervently. Her beauty is as though indispensable to the prayer. Night invades me. The moon is round, full of echoes. I think about the beauty of women and I want to write. But I won't because we are going to dance the beguine. Move hips, sway hips, birds of paradise, night is rhythm. And then Michèle says to me: "Look at that woman over there with her big hat, you might say, a black Djuna, a woman come out of nightwood, a heroine lost in her great love." I look at this woman and with her the world bends completely backwards.

9 March 1983

and with her the world bends completely backwards. Today the mother of my very best friend died. For Germaine, today will be a permanent today. A date as precise as the one when she emerged alive from the body of another woman.

Water, when the waters break and I'll know nothing about it, stretched out on the operating table, because Sesame, open up, flounders in wombs during caesarians and mothers sleep with exemplary soundness. Anaesthetized. Mothers in hospitals are hot, cold, tremble, revive, writhe, and bellow in rut. Mothers sign with a big X over the eyes of their children, sign the end of the eternal recommencement when they leave the hospital or when they leave reality or when they leave with a big X on their bellies. Yes mothers have all the attractions and all the trumps for the Xs that dance in their eyes, mothers have obligations, rendezvous, mothers draw inspiration from the deepest silence. Mothers suddenly desire the sea and the salt just like the amazons, gazing on the sea, must have tasted the salt of their lovhers as reality, mothers become grave and gravitate around their centre of gravity and then float, aerial, mothers who invent humanity in inventing their daughters in their own image and in the fuzziness of this image, mothers invent their life like tigresses, mothers put fire in the eyes of the she-wolves on the uttermost patriarchal steppes and the she-wolves become women in the crystalline curve of humanity. When this has been accomplished, the mothers say they have no time to keep their journals. Only their voice is heard then and their voices are never quite their own voice. They are voices that have travelled to the horizon like little clouds. And life gets ordered in spite of their sentences of love, and life erases their sobs.

24 April 1974

I see you, I look at you. Intensely is only a word. It's love at first sight, body and soul a whole life long. Bolt from the blue, light, energy. Your life to come. You are my daughter one day where the real and the fiction overlap. You are the one called La Capucine and through you the world is an April day radiant in your black hair. My sweet downy girl, I dreamed you were born already knowing how to speak.

14 March 1983

Montreal sunny. A luminosity full of vibrations. Almost spring in the clothes. They're all quite sombre this morning, in mourning, in tears, people dressed in black. It's the day of the funeral. At the church, an entire childhood resurfaces, the music of *Kyrie eleison*, the smell of incense. Then total revolt when the priest opens his mouth. Everything he says is gendered masculine: men, brothers, the son, sons, the father, fathers. It's difficult. It's unbearable, it's odious when you say goodbye to a woman and hand her a servant's apron.

In the Metro, I try to forget the mourning, my sadness, and I continue reading *Des filles de Beauté* but where I've reached on page sixty-six I happen upon a burial not far from where I lived for the first five years of my life. De Lanaudière, Beaubien, those were streets not to be crossed. In the metro, a woman wears a button on her black coat and Van Gogh stares at me with his air that was thought to be mad, the madman's look in his self-portrait, his air of resemblance, his intimate-journal look. And I say to myself that art is a refuge when you have the time or it is not too late. And I say to myself it is not too late to return and write my journal. The day is still young. The weather is fine in the No. 51 bus at the corner of Saint-Laurent and boulevard Saint-Joseph and the light is going to change, for sure, you can't spend a whole life on red. And suddenly it comes back to me: in front of the church porch the beauty of the petals of the birds of paradise strewn on the ground. Then I wondered whether there was any relation between Martinique, death, and going to paradise.

Yes, to all this, I've dreamed for a long time of trying to ruse with reality while thinking about being able to live in the deferral of the virtual, leaving Paris-Carotte to her fate on page sixty-nine of *Des filles de Beauté* and forgetting the redheaded woman who was picking up the coffee cups in the garden of the chateau of Cerisy-la-Salle. I still think about all this while saying to myself that it was a single episode and the day was not going to end then for all that, no more than life, moreover.

enough say everything in the closest second rustle moves which (hi)story the fictionalized biography in a chateau a notebook dreams/dies with insomnia my dayfall in snatches seduces one a red-headed woman who laughs writing surprised by the voyage so much beauty the seaside and ferns other readings of the subject bio-life prow child the echo of birds in a bed signs surprise the fuzziness of the image orders the sentences of love blotter the light is going to change mused while saying to myself continue art is a refuge life too late candle lit beautiful dresses body prodigious with audacity in your black hair a whole life I write in my notebook a half-hour of reading <u>for real a glance</u> blinding life turns on a few words

who laughs writing prow child
life too late
in a bed other readings
so much beauty seaside
i'll write the subject in snatches
beauty seaside blinding

3

18 March 1983

Yesterday, it was a matter of remaking the world as it is today, moreover. Yesterday, the world was a hypothesis as a future. Yesterday, it was what I didn't do and what in the future I would perhaps have done, or will do, or it will do, *ferai ou fera,* the ferry that takes us to the island.

Greece, Skiathos, 15 July 1973

I never expect anybody when I'm on an island. Yesterday, I was on the mainland at Volos. Volos, that I shall never forget because yesterday was a night of sex, alcohol, and deadly passion. Yesterday, I had thought about living with a woman as one flies above the plain of Messara, with one's whole body trembling, future and winged for eternity.

Between Volos and Skiathos, the light, the ghosts of the night before, the fishermen's little blue boats, salt burning lips. On the boat, between Volos and Skiathos, we threw our gold rings into the sea, after having put them in our mouths so as to liberate them from a bad fate. Athens' owl sinks into the water at the same time as Minerva. The gold owl reflected the daylight before disappearing. Between Volos and Skiathos, I know that my life was at stake and I wasn't the one gambling it. Nobody faces death without confronting life. Voyages come to an end. I never expect anybody when I'm on an island. O how memory surfaces quickly in an intimate journal. Those mountains you cross after two hours driving, holding hands when there is no twist or turn in the road or when the curves are those of our ample and inconsequential gestures like a kiss going around a bend. All curves are lesbian when inventing a return to the self in the most audacious way, raising an eyelid and then closing it while embracing eternity. Who's there? It's me, me completely, and the curves are approaching at top speed like the end of the world, you remember, the end of the world was at the end of a woman on a tightrope. But no, the end of the world is the end of a man at his limits in the retrospective

of men's humanity, the end of the world is a crack in men's
heads that makes the world shatter with a single <u>smile</u>, with a
single hand. Tell me, woman of Volos, you will not surrender
in the shade of the olive trees, at the foot of the Meteors, tell
me no monk will take you up into his fortress in his tourist
pony cart, tell me, woman of Volos, your memory does not
begin with a reading of Plato. Bold patriarchy camouflaged in
the perfume of jasmine. Dance, dance then a little more.
Dance and smile, dance, dance again a while. Dance and con-
sume yourself.

19 March 1983

Yesterday the world needed to be remade. Yesterday, like today,
is a very quiet day with no troubles; you need only look outside. The city is always ready for anything that will give pleasure. The city is filled with celebrities and nobodies. Today, I'll
go and walk in the parks and streets that are beginning to
smell spring-like as they did in New York in 1975, when Luce
Guilbeault and I discovered feminist America and we knocked
on all the doors in order to make a good film. Bouquet of
flowers in hand to comfort Ti-Grace Atkinson with the flu, a
big smile and nervousness to interview Kate Millett. Or again
with a certain scepticism we waited for the elevator to stop at
the twenty-fourth floor to meet Betty Friedan. New York,

passion, curiosity, swept us off our feet. Telephones, rendezvous, performances, bookstores, the shabby premises, the
big meetings, sandwiches with a marxist flavour on one side
and feminist on the other. Counters overflowing with beautiful fruit forbidden to the street people, weak, old, and sad.
New York is filled with sunshine. The yellow taxis cast light-
ning bolts in their path. The new American feminist cuisine at
Mother Courage restaurant. And the fat woman at the next
table makes me blanche with fear until I remember that, in
the film *The Honeymoon Killers,* she was the one who lured the
victims into the death trap. To settle the question between
reality and fiction once and for all, I approach her and invite
her to our table. It's really her, Shirley Stoler. She's the fat
woman again in the next film of Lina Wertmüller, she tells us.
Fiction, reality. And Luce who has also played so many roles.
Fiction: the doubling, identity or synthesis of the real.

Let's forget about bodies and concentrate on voices and the
gaze. Why forget the body? Because at that time, the body
could too easily be confounded with the collective history of
all those women's bodies seeking a soul. Or was it a secret soul
that made me mix up all the silent women into one body?
Those women who spoke had a soul of course and that was
what we were looking for. Soul sisters who could explain the
world to us in the feminine.

One evening, coming back to the hotel, an image came to me
of two parallel societies: men's society and women's society.
Each of them had their own hierarchy, their little and great
miseries. I was troubled, very troubled, and I tried with a great
many drawings, graphics, and scales of value to understand
how to avoid hierarchy, the abuse of power, the little and great
miseries. It was difficult and tiring and yet I have not stopped
trying to understand ever since; not society but what is hidden in thought, how thought works to bring into being the
society we know and are subject to. All that consumed a great
deal of energy and despair too, especially when it comes to
writing all that or about it all. But I had an advantage: I could,
in writing, slow down the act of writing. I had always done
that. Slowing down between each word I learned to identify
a certain number of the technics of thought. I also learned to
see the gaps coming, to hear them without ever being able to
make myself quite their echo. The blanks, what are called
white spaces, are in fact so full of thoughts, words, sensations,
hesitations, and audacities that it can all be translated only by
a tautology, that is to say, by another blank, a visual one. It is
in the white space that anybody who writes, trembles, dies,
and is reborn. Before and after the blank space everything
goes well, because there is the text. And it fills up a life so well,
a text does! Every text is a sample, that is to say a small amount
displayed in order to give an idea of the whole. A text serves

as an example. And each text is exemplary too, because it bears witness to a process of thought, in its simplest expression as in its most explorean trajectory.

Paris, 27 November 1975

Yesterday, the world needed to be remade again. Luce and I are continuing our work begun in New York. But this time, we're in an autumnal Paris. It's my birthday. In an hour, I interview Simone de Beauvoir about American feminists. Has the author whose *The Second Sex* was an illumination for the women who became radical feminists been inspired in turn by these women capable of smashing the partriarchal lie?

I was worried, because the day before I had seen an interview Simone de Beauvoir had granted to French television. I had been disappointed. Not by her words but by the dutiful daughter. No body; only a mouth that moved, and sometimes her hands approved, rising lightly, imperceptibly above her knees. Let's forget the body, I had thought in New York, but today I didn't want to forget anything.

Yesterday is so alive and present in Paris. Paris is yesterday at every street corner. We are walking, camera and sound recorder on our shoulders toward Montparnasse. Visual, sonorous, all the senses are kindled in a flash. We shoot. We ask questions. And then, one day, this footage, very short, disappeared as though it had all never existed. Disappeared how? Mystery at the National Film Board. Travelling shot in the corridors, in the cafeteria. No zoom in prospect. Yesterday, a little while ago, soon no history.

Athens, 20 June 1973

I must pay attention not to mix up my notebooks, those in which I exist and those in which I write. Those where there is heroism and those in which the heroines rewrite the text. I mustn't confuse the sexes and I must be able to contradict myself. As Clarice Lispector wrote: "I'm almost free of my mistakes."

The heat. The silence at siesta time. Silence and yet the marble that amplifies the least sound, the slightest whisper.

19 March 1983

I must have thrown out all my notes because I am unable to find them again. I have looked everywhere in my drawers. Still the afternoons in Athens, I remember them. Our fear and anxiety while walking on Bouboulinas Street, where we knew the colonels' men were torturing people. I probably lost the notebook, the one in which I described the scrawny and mangy cats who roamed around our table in Heraklion. I undoubtedly left the notebook in the bar in Mykonos or on rue Duluth before going to pick up the proofs of *French Kiss.* Yesterday, it's not very precise in time, it's like the echo but the echo of our voices in the theatre at Epidaurus was very clear. How beautiful and sexy we were in our summer dresses, with our skin tanned everywhere even in the finest creases. We were great singers and supreme in our hope of remaking the world. Yes, but I lost that notebook at the same time as I forgot the name of the great philosophers. I lost the echo of the echo and today, I must remake the world from a few sounds; several sounds if I think in the past, all possible sounds if I think in the future.

Delphi, 30 June 1973

I'm close to the oracle, Athena and the others. The sky will be blue just like in my next novel. I am focusing on the incoherent words of the Pythia. I interpret her cries. I am a priest, I become Freudian, I am ready to take beautiful pictures that I'll develop myself in my dark room. We are going from ruin to ruin. We stop and someone translates everything we need to know. In spite of our cameras filled with impressions and temples, I buy a few postcards and we go back to the hotel to make love, in a place where nobody else will interpret our incoherent words and the sounds we make.

19 March 1983

Yesterday I thought that in a creative-writing workshop there ought to be at least one writing exercise with the words: window, drawer, and mirror. After, we'll see! Yesterday "maman died," yesterday "everything swallows me," yesterday "Cuba sinks in flames," yesterday a text begins like this. Yesterday, ante, haunted. The past haunts me in the intimacy of the journal. What exactly do you want from me? Literature that won't look like literature? Writing that will not be writing? <u>Do you want me to look cute</u>? Memoirs, autobiography, journal, fiction. O! of course, you need to differentiate them, but who is to do that?

New York, March 1980

The carpet of the Barbizon Hotel for Women is well worn. The walls a sad green and somewhat grey. The Barbizon Hotel for Women is an old hotel and most of the women who live there all year or who stay there temporarily have more or less aged along with it. In its early days, it was a hotel for young women of good families. A hotel for women only. No men in the rooms. That reassured parents who were paying for their daughters' studies in big, threatening New York. <u>No room for King Kong</u>.

At the Barbizon, more than anywhere else, today is well and truly yesterday. With a beautiful ball room for Saturday night and perhaps Guy Lombardo and his orchestra all smart, blaring, rousing, lulling future lawyers and future mystified women. Mystified the feminine must well have been and medusified, too, those girls who received a diploma in one hand and with the other gave their life in exchange. At that time, women gave themselves body and soul. Women slaved even when they weren't working. Something was working in their heads, ringing, stamping, bending, it exhausted the women in their heads to have to forget everything they had learned in the classrooms, the big gymnasiums, the laboratories and in friendship.

New York, New York. <u>I love New York</u> and the art galleries and museums and the culture at auctions. American school, women's school. Everything gets mixed up in my head. I persevere and work hard to express myself. It will soon be time to go and lie down and invent a future in the narrow beds of America.

20 March 1983

Yesterday it would perhaps have been better for me not to go out. I went walking on Mount Royal. I should perhaps have gone to rue Saint-Denis where I could have met Yolande Villemaire, France Théoret, Pauline Harvey or a girl from *La Vie en rose*. We would have begun by talking about the beautiful day, then about a coffee or beer to order, then about the book Sollers dared to title *Women* in the plural, or again, we would have returned to the subject in talking about the success of International Women's Day last March 8th. One of us would have said that the latest issue of *La Nouvelle Barre du jour* was excellent, then little by little we would come to the point of showing each other some book bought just a while ago at the Librairie Androgyne. We would have smoked five cigarettes for one beer, ten for two, and a whole package with the fourth. Another woman would have bought a Perrier with lemon, and still another would have asked for news of Julie Capucine and I of Claude or Jean-Paul.

Yesterday, I'm not expecting anyone. Yesterday, is like an island. It's an island that disappears then re-appears. Yesterday is a sleeping volcano. At that time, it's like today, with a mountain slope transformed by fire. A slope of the lunar landscape after having spit out fire. And the other slope, the untouched side? And the other slope?

It would have been better for me not to go walking on Mount Royal. But all that, the walk and the reverie, I only did that in order to write. It's a closed circuit: I don't go out because I must write and I'll have nothing to write if I don't go out. I need to go to the gynecologist, the dentist, to the department stores, I must go to Radio-Canada for an interview, I have to make an appointment for lunch at the Café Laurier, and I should call my mother, I must pick Julie up after her ballet lessons. It's so beautiful outside, such good weather. Just the same I'm not going to begin to write down everything that's running through my head. I no longer recognize myself.

I feel as though I am going to end up saying everything and the Id, it's not very interesting. At any rate, one can never say everything. There are gaps, spaces. Blanks are inevitable. In painting, in music, in writing, the white space is de rigueur. The blank space is inseparable from fiction and from reality. Through the white space we engage the circumstances of writing as if entering into the invisibility of our thoughts. Others call white the void we need to fill in order to get to know society. Or again white, the vibrant luminosity that is eventually separated into the vividness of anecdotal colours. Blank of absence, white of full presence. One always has to begin again, like a particular day we'll observe, a holiday, when the world is unravelled all around us.

yesterday the world in the rhythm of the hypothesis on an
island the body in the night of sex trembles caresses gushes
before disappearing completely made me lesbian of curves
break breach braise of kiss my synthesis of the real all that
energy sensation speech and knee angles of perception no
body or all body at siesta time the heat echo of the echo if i
think in the future i forget names you have to differentiate
invent derive from the book exhaust the slope nuances of
honey the courage of fiction that is confounded fundamen-
tally with a film it's white all that it's blinding to be subject to
white vivid white all white troubling after seeing that yesterday a text sinks in flames and swallows me up to begin from
here women's opinion in prose lemon water café i no longer
recognize myself obegin by observing how vacillates oscillates
near the eyelashes in the island fairy-like life make me muse

curve break braise my synthesis
of the real all that sensation
white all white troubling
oscillates near the eyelashes
life make me muse

4

25 March 1983

Everything's a question of framing in the landscape of the real, of montage and dissolve in memory, when a mental frame is transformed into a precise image of a woman in the process of writing. In contrast, you have to expect the real twice because there is no real(ity) except the science of being as an absolute necessity otherwise consciousness does not survive, invisible in the montage.

26 March 1983

I write with my eyes. Eyes are for memory the obstacle that endlessly renews. Thrown back on itself, memory revolves around itself like another phenomenon one must try to grasp. I concentrate often on what I can see as though to lighten things and sum up time; I concentrate in order to perceive only what carries me beyond the field of reality. But then, I mustn't forget the way back or rather each time reinvent a new route that will take me back to reality. There is no free circulation of thought if thought is restricted to retracing itself, always using the same imaginary landscape. Every day, I have to risk new mental positions otherwise I founder in the anecdotal or else I linger over facile equations of the type this equals that or that does not equal that.

Budapest, 19 June 1978

Four o'clock in the afternoon. Popular café. Women and men converse in a language unique in the world. A language that makes every Hungarian poet, man or woman, a translator. Paul Chamberland tells me about the Egypt he dreamed and about the cosmos. Sometimes, we grow silent and we write. I don't know why, but this scene of two poets writing without reticence in front of each other has only happened to me with male poets (Chamberland, bpNichol, Roger Des Roches). I have nonetheless travelled with women writers, but it is as though the act of writing could not find anchorage in the eyes of the other woman. The spoken word signifies all sensations; speech engages emotion.

At the back of the room, a young woman is writing. I am always fascinated by a woman who writes; I mean that she is physically there, really in the process of writing. I could invent a love story with this woman. Bodies work at surviving so as to inscribe differently the intense animation that questions their slightest gestures. Poet is *költo* in Hungarian. I asked our guide, the beautiful, young and innocent Katalin, if there were feminists in Hungary. She replied no but that there was a woman minister. I understood then that I knew all the answers to my questions about women. Anyway, women are workers who sometimes give birth and there are statistics for that.

Tomorrow, we'll follow the curves of the Danube. Today, we bought Hungarian blouses for our daughters. Tonight, we are going to hear *Falstaff* at the opera. After, we'll go to another café and the men will get drunk with their eyes full of tears until they collapse into the arms of a friend. And the women will get drunk and lose their make-up. And the mascara will stream slowly down their cheeks. Balinka. Balinka. The violinist rests his head on his violin. It is very late and tomorrow we are leaving for Balaton. Before going to sleep, I'll read a few poems by Agnes Nemes Nagy translated by the poet Guillevic and others by Anna Pardi that I transcribe in my notebook:

> Since I've grown up
> I've made a habit of looking at the sun
> of not fearing fear
> of giving myself limitlessly to every limit
> with permission to enjoy the body fully.

Balaton, 23 June 1978

Balaton is a big lake. A small inland sea. A summer resort. We are visiting. We are resting. I have no emotion to add to the landscape. All the poetry is in another notebook. I am neither sociologist nor psychologist. Life is lived full stop, that's all. Sometimes I lie like a lizard in the sun, sometimes I walk in the village streets, sometimes it's like in an old Hungarian legend in which the Milky Way is called the armies' road. I listen to life lived. The East Germans think this place is the Côte d'Azur and they enjoy themselves greatly forgetting borders.

In Montreal, 26 March, I imagine Paris the 13th of April 1983

A month's absence from each other. It was a long time. Today I've found you again. I spent the whole month of March writing and thinking about you. All my love is in another notebook and I have no more energy left to write you. Today, we followed our usual itinerary the first day we're in Paris together. Lunch at Lipp's for prosciutto that reminds you of your childhood and of your little student's room in New York when you were longing for Italy. Lipp's makes me think of Les Deux Magots and a bit of the Madison hotel in my novel. Then we passed by Maryvonne's of whom I have often thought while writing my journal. Her journal is a daily affair and faithful to everything that haunts her and gives her joy. After visiting Maryvonne, we took the Metro to the Museum of Holography which I wanted to see again. Its location has changed for the third time. No great novelties but holography always fascinates me. Then we met one of your friends. An intellectual a bit too snobbish for my taste. One of the type: "I am seriously thinking of becoming a radical feminist but you see..." I replied to her that it would deprive her of nothing, except the superfluous, the superficial, and the official. I tried to say it to her politely and I think I succeeded because it was as though all at once she started really speaking. I know she was really speaking before, but it added something racier to her gaze. It seems to me... Certainly, I may be wrong... It's a delicate matter, all that...

Later, Paris 13 April 1983

Leaning over reality, I look at the street. I see everything as far as the boulevard. I see the greengrocers and fishmongers. I see fresh meat. A merchant is digging in his pockets to find change. His customer waits, watching more or less attentively. Then she rummages nervously in her bag as if she were afraid of having forgotten something, or of having let it fall. There are patches of shadow on the sidewalk. I can't help thinking about all the novels I have read in paperback. The first to appear: Camus, Sartre, Giono, Mauriac. The landscapes, style, ideas, sensations. I remember rue Saint-Denis, long before it was asserted that to pinch things was to steal, all those covetted books in the Pléiade series. Irresistable books with the odours and scents of the *Odyssey*. Musty smell of lessons in Greek.

Two punks pass by and time remains unmoved. The world is performance, zero motivation, intersection, hallucinated sequences. Leaning over reality, I think about the show *La Mort du petit bonhomme en noir*, the one who jumped into the abyss in order to shatter reality without splitting his skull one Sunday in October, rue de la Commune. The body is staged, the body is ultimately much in view as post-modernity makes it central to everything. The body is nuclear, like an abandonment of everything. The body presses on all the red buttons without becoming alarmed.

In Paris, 13 April 1983, day cannot really come to an end. It is a premature day that I bring to an end nonetheless at an hour when like so many others I am in the twilight, between dogs and wolves. I move through the ancient streets. Eyes are for memory the obstacle that endlessly renews.

Montreal, 27 March 1983

A Sunday. A really real Sunday. Between the Laurier and Berri-de-Montigny stations, I took an inventory of everything as if I were preparing to write a novel, a real novel of four hundred pages with realist descriptions. A novel of realist sensations: the doors open, the doors close. A woman waits for the other metro. In her eyes fire is powder or beams, explosive or constructive. Sometimes you have to cross out the gaze so as to imagine the rest.

28 March 1983

It takes a minimum of concentration not to set the page on fire. I am in quest and in combat. I nurture my archetypes of the future. This combat is thought and the elucidation of what thinks it. Appearances, facts are important for me in as much as I am trying to trace the origin, the fiction that made them emerge and exist. As one assembles reality from pieces. Like a child's game of Lego but knowing that pieces are missing, knowing that some of them are invisible to the naked eye and that others are magnified a thousand times in my head and all around me. In the appearance of facts, I amplify the reality of appearance. Reality is an apparent certainty foiled by the textual real. So when I am walking peacefully in the city, I examine only one aspect of reality, one aspect of text, that is to say I question only my response to the universe. Reality is a long reply that never stops spreading out under our eyes like a text that stirs up all the questions one could possibly imagine.

29 March 1983

Everything is matter of sensations. From the Jacques-Cartier bridge, several fall in love. The material for sensations leaves nothing to forgetfulness. The material for sensations is a vital text that shakes up the impossible and the impossible emerges daily as everydayness. The material for sensations is incomparable.

30 March 1983

I reread a few poems written a week ago. I finished some reading that couldn't wait. I've done everything to try writing my journal. But how can one live for a journal? It's absurd. Man or woman, plotters all: Nin, Kafka, Gide, Woolf. In principle, one is alone, in principle, one is many. It's the principle that matters. Let's pretend that I am alone in my room or in a café or at the seaside. Imagine that nobody can read my thoughts. Imagine that all that is for laughing or crying. What does it matter to the world if I write that last night Michèle Jean came for supper at my place and we talked about computers and politics? If I relate how I met Alain Grandbois or Anne Hébert or Alfred Pellan? No, the question above all is what does it matter for me never to have met Djuna Barnes? What difference would it have made for me never to have met the woman of my life? How intimacy makes me laugh when I miss you so much and there are no intimate liberties to share.

Paris, 13 April 1983

You are sleeping while I'm the one who ought now to be dead tired and sleepy. How good it is to be with you again, to touch you, to watch you breathe. "Auprès de ma blonde qu'il fait bon rêver..."

Tango, tango. Carlos Gardel's records we bought at the FNAC. The little apartment on rue Saint-André-des-Arts. An old record player and miracle the room fills with music. We are abusing our power of concentration so much we can scarcely keep on our feet. Our steps, our gestures, our kisses, the embrace. We can barely stay on our feet while embracing eternity.

I look at the street. The curtain stirs a little. It's a beautiful day. You mustn't wake up now that I'm starting to write. But if you open your eyes, or even one eye, I shall not be able to stop myself coming to join you, wanting to invent everything again, caresses, silence, words, scents, the majestic glory of the Amazons. I concern myself with the unspeakable, with happiness, I am on the side of the unanticipated. I lay claim to everything, overcome with vertigo. Dizziness of a dazzling sight. I attend to everything: the clichéd, the habitual, and the unrecorded. I love it that we are so preciously pretentious with each other. The consequences are divine.

Paris, 14 April 1983

The day is getting on. It's nearly noon. The room is empty. A message for me to say that you will be back in an hour. I am already in search of events to narrate. But I know that you can't count on the everyday, it's too fragile. It doesn't take into account the voices working beyond everydayness. Those voices that make us levitate above everything after they have surged through us like an electric current. Voices which make claims on us beyond what we know, what we say, what we think we have to do during the day.

Today, let's begin at the beginning: breakfast. Go down to the café. Look at the people, the newspaper, the street. There aren't many children. I ought to telephone to Montreal to get news about Julie and my mother. She says that I never talk about her in my books. I find it difficult to speak about my mother in books and, moreover, it is always better to write thinking about oneself first. The self in the spiral of voices surrounding us, in the spiral of voices amplifying what I am in the urban sounds of intense moments of existence. Go down to the café. Turn my head toward the sun. See you arriving at a distance. Desire you. Hear your voice. Juxtapose the sounds, amplify eternity.

Paris, page 9, 15 April 1983

Loving you is not a restful thing. Loving you is a polysemic term deriving mainly from the sense that might be given to tension and concentration. Loving you is writing. I cannot do that distractedly or nonchalantly. Loving you and writing are simultaneous daily activities. They are two indissociable terms; not that your love or mine is a source of inspiration for me, but because loving you and writing stem from the same mental function, the same desiring circuit. The same economy. Loving you is thinking with my skin everything I am, in the unrecorded and re-commencing of words. *I love you* serves me as conclusion and introduction at one and the same time.

Page 10, 15 April 1983

Exhausting day. Poetry reading at the Maison de la Poésie. Long and captivating conversations in bistros. Telephone calls. Book purchases. Mild weather. Wild love. L'amour fou in the demand for silence and the absolute self.

Page 11, 16 April 1983

The journal isn't enough for me. It doesn't suit me. It's a form of writing that demands too much of me and not enough of what I am.

...

method. There's no method here. I have nothing to prove. I merely show myself. I read to myself out loud.

What kind of method would allow us to have in mind always a truth that even though fleeting would keep us in line? A method that would make us into a perfect equation. I have always imagined myself as an equation in motion in the night of time, undulating equation that approaches, that distances me, consigning me to vertigo and equilibrium, summoning me to bliss, to research, and urging me to conquest. I love to approach the preconceptions enveloping words dangerously because that forcefully obliges me to question everything: the provisional and the absolute. The provisional which is myself in this journal, in life, and the absolute that is I am.

17 April 1983

In Wittgenstein's *Blue Book* I read: "The answer is that the puzzles we try to remove always spring from just this attitude to language."

That is not the least affront for someone concentrating on language. It is, however, an inexhaustible source of reflection; it is perhaps there above all that any intiation begins enabling us to think about thought.

18 April 1983

I am seeking the attracting material that can make us sink into ecstasy.

an absolute necessity expect the real circulate freely among
the images in the process of writing this scene poetry concerns itself with everything tears intoxicate the cheeks streets
titles a warning the absence fascinates body that makes an
effect novel cross out pageless in the metro eyes are book
lovhers a real fright a step a back a step too many frightens
calculates the real climbing the stairs take aim at the obstacle
so much certainty for a single aspect of myself from the bal-
cony i examine the room the seaside how lucky i am to be
able to read in my thoughts in principle every woman is multiple back to the curtain eyes at the window let us say the day
existence some times some voices a message i love you i write
you the equation in the eye memory preconceptions memory a child's game a game i that's it imagined premature in
ecstasy a fluid body coming from the everyday to reach the
limit of voices

existence some times some voices
a real effect of fright
eyes at the window
a fluid body coming
from the everyday reaching
the limit of self

5

1 June 1983

Poetry is everything. Surge in the soul and instinct of our certainties, some certainties with which we obstinately commit ourselves, in the name of life and energy not to die in the midst of describing reality. Existing and co-existing. Can all that occur peacefully? In thoughts and in action.

From my window, I see the postman making his rounds. It's a mild day. There is some mail: three letters like three presences. One from Louise Forsyth who writes that no one has yet really understood *Picture Theory*. Then another from the poet James Sacré in which he writes me about poetry, lyricism, and texts to send him for the new periodical. *Oracl*. The third comes from a reader who asks me which of my books she should read first because her friends told her: if you want complicated poetry, read Nicole Brossard. There is also a post-card from Michèle Causse. Her writing encroaches on the caption which says: <u>Highway that goes to sea in the Florida Keys</u>. Postcards always make me dream: for the love of friend-ship. <u>For the soul</u>. A little kiss at the foot of the pyramids, a kiss in the Grand Canyon, tenderness, affection, <u>love</u>. In June, I prefer to go away. It's a diversionary tactic that helps me understand certain images or again certain sensations.

3 June 1970

London is grey. My suitcases heavy. Taxi. Thirty-nine Emperor's Gate is where my sister Francine lives in the London exile she chooses and loves every day. Perhaps because of our ancestors the English and my grandmother, Alice Gretham De Lorimier. I myself have taken after Chevalier de Lorimier.

Now it is tea time. I yield gracefully to this custom. A neigh-bour joins us in the tradition. She is a very distinguished old lady. She repeats the expression "<u>civilized people</u>" frequently and each time the entire British empire flies in my face.

In the evening, my sister and I go to a pub. Fog envelops us. A thick fog, a fog made for nights of horror, Jack the Ripper and Frankenstein. A romantic fog, too. London is suddenly filled with cliffs, surf, whirlpools, the sea surges, all that, I say to myself, so that the poetry remains in suspense in my head, so that I don't let go for a single second, both the dream and the temptation, and everything in me is translated by *once upon a time poetry.*

The cars' headlights give the night a hallucinatory air. We walk in the fog and the shadow of the fog in a country called London.

At the pub, we play a few games of darts. The beer is good.

6 June 1974

I live in a big house on the banks of the Rivière des Prairies. I have a two-month-old daughter. The land around the house is flooded. I write all that on a big red table where lie my daughter, my notebook, and my dictionary. A bouquet of red flowers whose perfume I'll never forget. Also in the house there are the smells of milk, diapers, and baby powder. Odours that diffuse poorly in a formalist text. Poetry is to be found somewhere in the flooded garden.

6 June 1975

From the airplane, New York is a big cemetery with all its buildings shaped like tombstones. In the taxi that takes us to the Warwick Hotel, Luce Guilbeault and I continue discussing our feminist ideas. The voice of Elvis is suddenly interrupted by the victory of the New York Mets. The driver lights a cigarette.

7 June 1976

The stars. Everything is sensation. I am lost in the vast countryside of Abitibi. La Sarre is at the ends of the earth. After, it's the end of the world. In the hotel lounge, a woman is singing *J'ai un amour qui ne veut pas mourir.* The melancholy country-and-western melody always makes me forgive humanity everything, especially when she dances until <u>last call</u>.

Outside, the stars frighten me at the end of the world, the stars give me the impression of being nowhere, and yet of being on watch in the night.

It's the cosmos as far as can be seen inside my head. Everything that I haven't read and that I haven't written suddenly catches fire like a comet, a falling star in my head, words are cut short and my body is on edge and my body stretched out in the grass tries to guess what instinct it could be when we feel ourselves dying little by little in the unrepresentable as in an abstract part of the self, dazzled and burning among the scents of the night.

10 June 1977

Moncton. Work as a researcher on the custom called Charivari or Shivaree, as they say here. Memramcook Valley. Flood of words. Shots of gin around the kitchen table. Flood of words. In Moncton, La Cave à Pap is filled with poets who also remember everything without sacrificing in any way the reality of sleepless urban nights. That night, I heard the tidal bore breaking behind the hotel, long wave under the full moon. I am watching along the coast, close to the sea. My notebook is full of tenderness for the Leblancs, the Chiassons, the Légères, the Savoies...

13 June 1979

Assiduously and imperturbably I skirt around the forms of life. I divert everything into poetry while by-passing my life, my women friends, my loves. I even get around the spiral: I'll get the better of myself only in excess, carried away by the poem. At the limit, I remain imperturbable.

15 June 1980

June, the fever. All utopias are synchronized in our gestures of love. In our voices (the voice that Roland Barthes calls an organ of the imaginary), in our voices, theory serves all emotions.

June 1981

Mexico. I'm here for the Fourth Conference of Interamerican Women Writers. I'm in the courtyard of the Palacio de Medicina, in the scars of the Brazilian women, in the perfume of the beautiful bourgeois women from Argentina, I'm here in the cocktails; I'm here at the Folkore Ballet of Mexico, I'm here in the little café where women get together to listen to tangos, I'm here in the workshop on Quebec literature, I'm here in the plenary but, we'll say, we'll always be missing a few signatures to eliminate the violence that scars bodies and lacerates the pages of history, our pages of liberty.

20 June 1982

Paris. Hotel Madison. Boulevard Saint-Germain is filled with
thousands of demonstrators. Protesting nuclear arms, against
the madness of war. Against death. During this time, Julie and
I go looking for the greatest painters and their masterpieces.
It's with great pride that I enter the Louvre arm in arm with
my daughter. The stars: Leonardo da Vinci and the Egyptian
mummies. In the evening, we're going to Muniche and Julie
will devour the fire-eaters with her eyes, the clowns, the
accordion players, the big gypsies with their feverish gaze.
Tomorrow, we're going to Geneva, then to Milan, then
Barcelona, then everything will continue tranquilly like at the
seaside and we'll stretch out to infinity by closing our eyes.
At Denia, the afternoons are scorching. Around me, reality
begins to falter. I decide not to count the days. I number my
notes like temporal ellipses.

Note 21

Lyricism is perhaps when something sprawls so that it is no
longer recognizable, and yet on its own is going to catch us
unaware further on, from as far, so far in the repetition that we
learn to give up the superfluous.

Note 22

Today, the word's inevitable in a journal. A sort of accompanying refrain that incites us to raise high the colours of the emotion of the moment. Today, at this end of the month of June 1983, I sum up what I have written so as to pursue other writing projects. Poetry, I'm returning to it, never leaves me. It's my genre completely. In poetry I contemplate myself exuberantly. It's my unique strength. Force of gravity, electric and magnetic energy; in my own way, to make a synthesis. To make consciousness as, it is said, to make love.

Note 23

What makes me believe that I am writing a poem when I write a poem? What certainty can I have that it's really a poem and not something else that in my mind would, however, not be lacking poetry?

Note 24

This holiday's a bit like remembrance day. Some times my child's eyes are immersed in fleecy white wool, others my adult gaze shows up on the streets of Old Montreal.

By looking obliquely, the eyes of the politicians have dimmed. There will be no country, there'll only be songs for the old boys of Collège Brébeuf and Collège Sainte-Marie.

Note 25

At what moment does something in the mind become unreadable, unfit for use, or unthinkable in any way other than what makes it readable? Can one translate what in the mind confronts the unspeakable or again what in the body confines us to the inexpressible within the symbolic field?

There are days like today when my thought works only in the interrogative mode. That makes a change from the peremptory assertions which, I don't hide it from myself, are necessary for the work of discernment I carry out afterwards.

Note 26

Here I am. After working hard for so many days to make a pretence of telling about myself, here comes the foreseeable and dreaded sadness. For settling to the task of looking in detail at what makes a life, only returns one to the basic constant of solitude, to the grotesqueness of boredom like the woman passing in front of my window with two pekinese entangled in their leash. A sad image, this psychoanalytic trio.

For someone who is not talkative by nature, the journal is the very bottom drawer of existence. I always knew that and that's why I always fled those places, those moments, those books where someone confides, where someone confesses the little remaining, I mean the essential, like a time-bomb. You have to be insane to confide the essential to anyone anywhere except in a poem. Even in the greatest intimacy, one has no right to empty out the bottoms of the drawer.

I only consent to reveal my dreams in the intensity of pleasure, in the zero degree that threatens all interpretations and yet initiates them like so many dreams.

Note 27

It is late. Four o'clock in the morning. S. and I are coming back from the grand going-away party Louise gave for Monique. It took place in a big garden all in bloom. Music, dance, and conversation. It all happened in the bodies as if by magic. Each body was a limitless erogenous zone. Each woman was a forest, a flower, a perfume as in myths. I didn't have the energy to invent different imagery. I relied on the happiness of the senses and that was more than enough for me. Each woman in her own way invented gestures at the same time as the intonation of her voice. Instead of getting lost in each other so as to produce the illusion of blending, the voices all drifted towards each other in a fair approximation of the libidinal.

Almost all the women I had known over the last ten years were present. This evening, my senses were affected only by presence and perfumes. Names didn't matter much, nor the content of conversations. For once, I let myself be lulled by what lulls, amused by what amuses, and enchanted by what enchants. Lightly brushing the bloom of flesh. Everything on the surface. And it was delightful, restful, and would last as long as I wanted it to. I didn't ask any questions, I didn't answer any. It was my way of pursuing my thoughts in the privilege of a night of plenitude.

Note 28

Intense moments. Fine writing. Desire ever more. That's really good. Expression adjusts itself to sensation. Desire is ever more embodied. The universe recommends it, recommences it, and with my language I insist on it. Lyricism? To think it, I learn not to exceed on the margin, to pretend not to see her thigh from below. Yes, I know, it is not only that. But nothing now can stop me doing it in my head. Now when I write the word thigh, it's too late, she obsesses me, exhausts me, her skin, especially its softness, and nevertheless my hand slides, runs along thigh, face, cheek to cheek, in broad daylight. Wanting even more, embody. It's good like this. Maybe I won't write anything today, it's quite pleasant the state I've reached, it's like experiencing a feeling yes I know that combines with the desire, the contour, the roundness, a certain warmth at the fingertips that doesn't allow any more reflection. Another minute. Wanting more and more.

Note 29

Yesterday, I should not have written the word thigh. It's because of the word thigh, I know very well at which place. The word came to me just like that, without paying too much attention. It is true that I had used the word lyricism a few lines before, but that explains nothing. It is true that I have written a great deal in the last few days and perhaps I dimmed the lights on what I would naturally have been tempted to call the bloom on my skin.

For the moment, I must give up the effect that it had on me. I must think, I must think seriously to write.

Note 30

It's not the end of the world when you finish a notebook. There will always be burning, unspeakable, tormented, and sovereign desire. And its fulfillment each time with no other delay than to realize effects of the real in full consciousness.

There will be other inscriptions, other descriptions, other narrations, and that will all serve as a tactic of diversion. And I'll swerve each time it seems necessary. I'll demand short improvisations just as I'll submit to the long sessions of work in the autumn mornings, or in the blinding frost of winter, or again I'll insist on rereading certain things on summer evenings, sitting in the garden, my hand resting calmly on your thigh. All that to enable me to measure the distance between today and the fact of beginning to write again. All that in order once again to try to understand everything, even the impossible. But nothing is impossible except two or three badly written sentences.

Tomorrow, it's July eternity and that compels me to all the dazzle of adornment just as to the greatest humility in the vertigo that makes me want to remake the world every time.

Tomorrow I'll manage to plunge into the course of events again. There'll be some precise memories that will come back to me like some readings and with a déjà-vu in style. Tomorrow, there's a long metamorphosis of the mind and consciousness, a matter with the radical consequences of an exacting transition. Today, it comes back to me that to exist is always what catches us by surprise.

Tomorrow don't ask me what was, what will be my life. Tomorrow, there'll be my appalling claim to lucidity.

surge in the soul poetry certain instinct tranquilly <u>for the soul</u>
writing encroaches for the love of sensations shadow of shadow cliff at the end of the night the garden surf poetry is to be
found somewhere in the garden everything is sensation even
humanity poetry my lovhers at the foot of the pyramids
tomorrow tango tomorrow thighs i note this evening at the
end of the world desire more embodied tomorrow in the sun
it's foreseeable desire improvises your work without knowledge of everything of lack and excess there is silence it's an
exit degree zero <u>for the soul</u> so many readings dizzying dazzle of adornment it's elementary tomorrow autumn wanting
more and more

the poem is certainty
representing me
dizzying dazzle of adornment
elemental women wanting more
and more

Works of Flesh
and Metonymies

For Julie and Léa Nicole

Bellies

The two women hadn't seen each other for seven months. One September morning flaming with ochre and burgundy, the younger woman had left for Europe, perhaps the Alps, the Black Forest, or a grey city beside the Baltic Sea. Far away, she would learn a foreign language and life would unfold. Today, the young woman has come back four months pregnant. In a few weeks, she would leave again for another place and her destiny.

Three times a day she caressed her belly, rubbing it with sweet oil that, she said, would allow the skin to stretch as much as needed, then regain its elasticity, its initial form with the delicate radiance of youth.

In her gesture there was a happy mixture of determination and infinite tenderness. Twenty years earlier, the other woman had also given birth, but it seemed to her that she had forgotten everything: the nausea, the waddle, the enormity of it all. In the depths of her memory she retained only the sudden euphoria that had given her the impression of being launched at high speed into the cosmos and its landscape riddled with metaphysics. Moved, as though suddenly illiterate and voiceless before the repeated phenomenon of the belly, reputedly eternal, she was content with looking at the young woman through the mirror of time, musing upon the succession of pregnant women throughout the history of art and representation. Sculpted bellies, enormous in stone and wood, bellies sleeping under the folds of gold and purple robes of the Renaissance. Peasant bellies. Bellies of *The Lady Weighing Pearls* and the woman with the modern expression in Vermeer's *Woman in Blue Reading a Letter.* Bellies of pensive women.

The Garden

During the same year, the two women saw each other again, in the East this time. On the other side of the Atlantic. The young woman now spoke a foreign language that she alternated with the mother tongue linking her to the other woman. They were sitting in the garden. Around them, summer reigned with the sounds of cicadas and crickets, the perfume of roses and azaleas. Their soft voices floated above the grass and flowers. They were astonished that their voices were so rich in echoes and intonations.

"I'm expecting a girl," the young woman said delightedly. It was culturally possible for her to think it natural that nothing could be more joyous than to give birth to a daughter. To want a girl and to declare it loudly was a recent phenomenon limited, nonetheless, to a tiny part of the globe. Elsewhere still daughters were a source of humiliation for fathers, a burden and by-product of humanity. So they got rid of girls before birth, during childhood, adolescence, or even later if they became infertile wives or incapable of producing sons. Girls, women, disappeared, burned, decapitated, strangled, sold, or simply abandoned to the cold and hunger.

In the garden, night fell. The older woman could not manage to conceal her emotion. The young woman took her hand, placed it on her belly. The mother dissolved in tears, incapable of uttering any words when her feelings made everything tremble, collapsing the arrangement of roles everywhere. Mother tongue was a pang, the ultimate oath of allegiance. Inalterable language.

The Salon

The young woman had grown up surrounded by intellectual and creative women. Every Thursday afternoon, her mother's living room filled with women's voices. Smiling, sometimes noisy, each woman on entering had a gesture, a word, a kiss for the three-year-old who ran about the room. During the meetings, sitting on her mother's lap, the girl drew while the women debated, grew excited, laughed sometimes very loudly. Sometimes one of the women cried and the voices would change into murmurs and whispers. Certain words reoccurred: feminism, patriarchy, violence.

Men sometimes came to the house. They had beards or mustaches. They asked the child's name, her age; then they took out papers, pencils, and big boxes as though they had come to play. They all repeated the same words: proofs to correct, deadline, layout, manuscript, launching, poetry, ideology, election, modernity.

Soon the little girl spent her days reading and writing as she had often seen her mother doing. Adolescent, she secretly read all the books written by her mother. As some dream of returning to the land of their ancestors, the girl searched for roots in her mother's books. At meal time, she often asked questions about men in general, followed by another about the truth concerning women's condition and customs. The mother, however talkative in the Thursday meetings, never knew what to reply, as though suddenly overcome by extreme modesty or placed before the impossible task of summarizing or simplifying the fruit of her reflection. These questions ought to have been addressed to the other women who came to the house. The mother could only recommend prudence, not too much, just what was necessary, so as not to frighten her daughter. It seemed to her that only books could bring the generations closer together and that only women outside a filial bond had the power to transmit culture and the ability to enlighten girls.

At a Distance

Once again, the moving away. The ocean. Cruel distance. Between the two women: telephone, fax machine, and email haven't succeeded in making up for the misfortune of being apart. Sometimes a letter, a book.

"I've revitalized *I*" thought the older woman. Also by day she wrote about aesthetics and ethics. But in the evening, on television, they all reappeared: thousands of hungry children who knows by what god in the midst of the women who were also hungry for life and peace nobody knows by what world order and, tribal chaos, mothers trample the dust as if they were burying the soul and future of their offspring. And always coming back to the rhythm of a morbid ad, the repeated image of an old woman going from war to war, from dictatorship to revolution, a scarf on her head, her hands chapped, her feet swollen, dragging herself along between the shrapnel, water bearer. Always the same old woman, the same tears, the same mouth open expressing terror and anguish.

One day at dawn, at the other end of the line, the voice of the young woman announced that her daughter Alexandra had been born in the middle of the night, bathed in her mother's clear blood like every child in the first moment of life.

The child makes us remember. Or maybe not. At any rate remember what? The repeated riddle of the flesh and its narratives in which each person gives herself up to the joy and fever of reordering everything so as to seduce the venerable species, the admired young who each time starts us off again in the hope of a better future.

Representation

The photographs began to arrive in eggshell coloured envelopes. Evidently, the young woman chose the stamps she put on each package with care, because they all bore the head of a woman. Women novelists, scientists, athletes and philosophers with piercing eyes succeeded each other on letter after letter like delicious winks addressed by the daughter to her mother.

Each photo was a little history of time, a veritable narration about the passage of slow hours and real time that transforms beings of flesh into disconcerting personalities. In the first photograph, her gaze blurred with mingled fatigue and joy, the young woman, like a fulfilled lover, an unspeakable pride alight in her eyes, holds in her arms: her perfect daughter.

Another photograph: mother, father, and child. Father and mother with eyes wet and red. Intimate and proud smile of mission accomplished.

Last photograph: the daughter alone, in diapers, Alexandra, girl-of-the-future, her face alert to the first fluttering of air on her skin.

Reproduction

She caught herself studying the child's face. Chin: the father's. Cheeks and forehead: the mother's. Eyes, for how long, are completely mine. The little fingers must be counted as though updating the family tree. Each body is a history of customs and ancient peoples telescoped into the present, the terrible succession of the present. In what urban night, in what linguistic labyrinth, on what information highway, will Alexandra's genes deposit their grain of salt, moving in the future of the species sometimes toward an encounter with ancient humanity, at others into the company of young cyborgs?

In what language will Alexandra construct her inner world, her utopian palaces and sites of belonging, her CD Rom of interactive emotions? Will Montreal have a place in her thoughts?

In her child's head, will the world begin to exist with a beautiful and terrifying book, will it begin with an image or sentence to become so much and so well desired that the girl will dare hurl herself body and soul into the fray, into the luxuriance of semantic chance and unforeseeable images in the imaginary that suddenly make reality oscillate in the ungloomy dimension of things? Undoubtedly, the world is simply going to begin again with the smell and heat of the maternal body, with the habit of voices and ambient noises.

(Mother)sea of Writing

"I have revitalized *I*, who am I then?" she wrote, thinking I must understand where the idea comes from that "forewarned is forearmed," that "a feminist is worth two women." Forewarned about *what* and why must she be worth two at the same time? Two so much alike that nobody dare separate them, or so different that nobody could confuse them any more. One speaking in the singular, the other in the plural.

Why two? To be better protected, to accomplish the double task of mind and body splendidly, or so never to be alone. Is a knowing woman condemned to seek her double, a soul sister or, divided forever, has she set off again with renewed vigour on a mad flight that sometimes comes nearer to the silent stars, sometimes lightly touches the (mother)sea and its continuous clamour? The zigzagging existence of a knowing woman.

What does the verb *to be worth* hide when a woman is involved? Should we speak of commerce, of exchange, barter, or plus-value? Is a knowledgeable woman a jewel, a pearl of a woman, or quite simply a flesh-and-blood woman whose lively senses make her fertile with imagination and courage?

Brilliant among her sisters who are less well-informed, whose courage is not debatable, however. Is the woman forewarned better suited to transmit her knowledge? What can she do for the generations of women to come? Is so-called feminine intuition enough to transform a girl into such a knowing woman?

Write me

On the telephone, the voices behaved normally. I'm well. And you? The baby and I are leaving soon for a holiday at Lake Constance. Yesterday, for the first time, I saw plane trees in a row like they were in my childhood books. I felt great joy touching their soft greenish-grey bark with its mysterious geography. Write me. I need the French language. I am experiencing a strange confusion in which French is surfacing again and the scenery of childhood: Côte-Sainte-Catherine, the schoolyard, the smell of the Christmas tree, and the emotion of the first snow transmitted from generation to generation, a kind of instinctual North. Plunge me again into the idea that literature is pleasure. The words roll about in my memory like children in the evening after school in the leaves of a golden autumn. Plane trees, chestnuts, baobabs. I have read so many books. We are all living on the edge of a *roman-fleuve*. Write me. Here the language is irregular. A syllable is removed and a complete word created, an ending added and the word turns our intentions inside out like a glove.

If you only knew how soft Alexandra's cheeks are. Every day, hugging each other, we travel among the foreign syllables of the language spoken here and we clear a little path for the future with the French words I whisper in her ear. Sometimes, with my warm breath, I place the verbs and exclamation marks in her little hands. In a similar impulse, the verb to imagine, and sometimes with the same breath three times joy between her fingers.

Write me. Be my mother a while longer. The time to read you and understand the truth women generally invent as solutions for happiness intoxicating the mind.

Sequel

Tell me what fascinates you. What would you like to be exposed to in the adventure of human relationships? To the intelligence, warmth, and diversity of your fellow creatures? I myself prefer to focus on understanding the rich mystery of chemical and physical laws that govern us and hold us breathless like creatures loving speed and dreaming the mind, sense within sense, in slowness and ecstasy under the dome of heaven.

The proximity of beings is troubling. Yes, it is true we change our expression at their approach, not knowing whether they wish us well or if their presence will bring us harm. Living in the company of others constantly displaces our centre of energy. Living alone suprises us even more.

Revitalizing *I* is perhaps only a grand form of superstition, a great luxury. In French, there is certainly a constant preoccupation with placing being at the centre of one's thoughts and stretching it like an elastic until it breaks.

Yes, undoubtedly one should love ordinary happiness so that life continues. Here, then. Yesterday, the beauty of snow falling slowly on Montreal. A bit of honey on my bread. Great thrill of love looking at the new photos of you and Alexandra. Later in the day, seeing January crack, "burnt by the deceptive sun," I took out an old book of world history and map of the globe. A simple thing always transports me to another place. Waves of (mother)sea.

Mother of a Man in December

In order not to trouble an innocent woman, I dare not write the name of her son, a misogynous murderer. In order not to overwhelm the mother, I must regulate the space between her and the name of the cursed son. Cut the tie. Pretend mother and son are different. The mothers are many but we know only the names of the son. So we never think about what they were like, *la mère de Gilles de Rais, die Mütter von Goering, math ot Staline, la mama di Al Capone, la madre de Pinochet,* the mother of Charles Manson. So many inconspicuous mothers and monstrous sons. Crossing out whoever erases her in saying *fils de pute*, son of a bitch, *hijo de puta*. Motherfucker!

The ties of blood. To spill blood. There was blood everywhere. Here even in a text of fiction, I dare not write the name of the son so as not to hurt the woman who gave birth to him.

Since that December.

There was blood everywhere in each century, as culture confirms. Woman, mother, girlfriends, daughters, wives, lesbians, waitresses, intellectuals, secretaries, lovhers, punks, topless dancers, farmers, feminists: none of the women understood why there was blood everywhere. But there was always fresh blood and the man ran faster than the blood in his veins.

The Culture of Feelings

Eyes plugged in to solitude, I watch January fall whiter and whiter. Schoolgirls cross the park. A woman walks her son. Over the centuries, periods and sketches, feelings are renewed according to fashion. Sometimes it's the reign of melancholy, of spleen, or hysteria, later fear of the sea or fire is cultivated, at another time the fascination for monsters and machines, anxiety over shipwreck and epidemic. Or nostalgia. We are enculturated through our fears and our desires. Accessories: handkerchief, fan, umbrella, cell-phone, laptop.

Habit makes time relative for us. At twenty, the faces surrounding us have no history except in the present of the gaze we turn toward them. So, young adults, old people, and children seem forever framed in a "just as I see you" that makes them impervious to change. Later, one discovers that faces and bodies are material for transformation. One guesses then that time's function is to pass very much alive like a current of heat and thought through the bodies gifted with this canny intelligence from which we learn to endow ourselves over the course of the years so as to repress elegantly the idea of death like the very last dregs.

That is how life stories are restored to us, since it is much easier to invent a past for each person than to imagine a future. Except for a few variants in the narratives, we are made to resemble each other in the long run. That is why we succumb so readily to fashion and the fascination we have for expressive faces.

Calendar of Appearances

nineteen hundred and thirteen birth of marguerite nineteen hundred and forty-three birth of nicole nineteen hundred and seventy-four birth of julie nineteen hundred and ninety-five birth of alexandra. The letter disperses over time. The number refers to History. 1913: *Swann's Way. Totem and Taboo. Fantomas* by Louis Feuillade. 1943: Uprising in the Warsaw ghetto. Fall of Mussolini. Construction of Los Alamos Centre. *Being and Nothingness. The Inner Experience.* 1974: Adoption of Bill 22. Resignation of Nixon. *Tableaux de l'amoureuse. Speak White.* 1995: Quebec Referendum. Peace agreement between Israel and Palestine. *These Festive Nights. Baroque at Dawn. Le Vent majeur.* End of the war in Bosnia. The war continues in Chechnya.

Girls' toys and children's joy vary according to science and industry. Marguerite had a rag doll, Nicole played with a wooden truck, Julie composed with the red and green letters of a plastic alphabet, Alexandra will have an interactive atlas where the ships of the Renaissance will be found alongside the Concorde and the trains of the industrial era. By pressing on a button, she will be able to awaken Vesuvius and make

California shake, set off white avalanches in the Himalayas. The index on <u>enter</u>, she will be able to displace entire populations and draw new boundaries. The names of the countries will scintillate at the same rhythm as the electrical flow of the human masses crossing the streets of megalopolises.

The century comes to an end bearing four generations of women toward new happy chance discoveries that will make the earth minuscule and children giants.

Write me again

I dream of being learned and happy. I dream of creating last-
ing bonds with humanity, between the ephemeral and the
beautiful. I know that you would like the future to be repre-
sented by the perfect daughter. The future can only lead us
back to the present of desire and necessity. The invisible flesh,
always hiding in wait in the belly, will create new bridges. Life
work and memory work, don't forget if you can, write me
again. I want to be learned but also to be able to take a rest
from the gossip and delirious noises that thinking beings pour
into language musing on eternity. Write me about ordinary
things that will make me feel tender and give me hope.
Prolong our walks on Mount Royal and Saint-Denis in gen-
tle words. Tell me about the spectacles that make Montreal a
permanent theatre. Embellish for me also with something
about the country. But don't repeat to me that there is a war
on and other universal contingencies. Let me dream, because
I am mobilized for the future. My daughter and I are already
on our way. From now on the world belongs to us. I have
decided. We will remain in solidarity with the Thursday
women of my childhood.

Intimate Journal
or
Here's a Manuscript

Journal intime was commissioned for a radio series by Radio-Canada. Begun January 26 1983 and finished March 28 1983, the journal was broadcast in French from August 8 to August 12 1983. Pol Pelletier read the journal and Yves Lapierre was the producer. My thanks to Jean-Guy Pilon who initiated this project.

My thanks to France Théoret who directed me to the quotations from Jean-Paul Sartre and Virginia Woolf.

The "postures" or gestures of text and the poems were written on September 9 1983 and the introduction on September 11 1983.

The translator thanks Carol for her alert ear and Beverley and Mitoko for their clever detective work.

Works Cited

Aquin, Hubert. *Prochain épisode*. Montreal: Le Cercle du Livre de
France, 1965. *Prochain épisode*. Trans. Penny Williams. Toronto:
McClelland & Stewart, 1967. p. 9.

Baillie, Robert. *Des filles de Béauté*. Montreal: Quinze, 1982.

Bataille, Georges. *L'Expérience intérieure*. Paris: Gallimard, 1943. *The Inner
Experience*. Trans. Leslie Ann Boldt. Albany: State University of New
York Press, 1987.

Blais, Marie-Claire. *Soif*. Montreal: Boréal, 1995. *These Festive Nights*.
Trans. Sheila Fischman. Toronto: Anansi, 1997.

Brossard, Nicole. *L'Amèr ou le chapitre effrité*. Montreal: Éditions du Jour,
1977. *TheSe Our Mothers* Trans. Barbara Godard. Toronto: Coach
House, 1983.

_____. *French Kiss: étreinte-exploration*. Montreal: Éditions du Jour,
1974. *French Kiss or A pang's progress*. Trans. Patricia Claxton.
Toronto: Coach House, 1986.

_____. *Baroque d'aube*. Montreal: Les éditions de l'Hexagone, 1995.
Baroque at Dawn. Trans. Patricia Claxton. Toronto: McClelland &
Stewart, 1997.

Brossard, Nicole and Luce Guilbeault. *Some American Feminists*. Canada:
NFB, 1976.

Camus, Albert. *L'Étranger*. Paris: Gallimard, 1942. *The Stranger*. Trans.
Matthew Ward. New York: Knopf, 1988. p. 3.

de Beauvoir, Simone. *Mémoires d'une jeune fille rangée*. Paris: Gallimard,
1958. *Memoirs of a Dutiful Daughter*. Trans. James Kirkup.
Harmondsworth: Penguin, 1959.

_____. *Le deuxième sexe*. Paris: Gallimard, 1949. *The Second Sex*. Trans.
H. M. Parshley. New York: Knopf, 1953.

Dekobra, Maurice. *La Madone des sleepings*. (1925). Paris: Livre de Poche, 1967.

Ducharme, Réjean. *L'Avalée des avalés*. Paris: Gallimard, 1967. *The Swallower Swallowed*. Trans. Barbara Bray. New York: Farrar Straus and Giroux, 1968. p. 5.

Freud, Sigmund. *Totem and Taboo*. (1913). Trans. James Strachey. London: Routledge & Kegan Paul, 1950.

Gagnon, Madeleine. *Le vent majeur*. Montreal: VLB Éditeur, 1995.

Gilman, Charlotte Perkins. *The Yellow Wallpaper*. (1892). New York: Feminist Press, 1973.

Guillevic. *Mes poètes hongrois*. 2nd ed. Budapest: Éditions Corvina, 1967.

Joyce, James. *Finnegans Wake*. (1939). Harmondsworth: Penguin, 1992. p. 74.

Lalonde, Michèle. *Speak White*. Montreal: Les éditions de l'Hexagone, 1974.

Lapointe, Paul-Marie. *Tableaux de l'amoureuse*. Montreal: Les éditions de l'Hexagone, 1974.

Lispector, Clarice. *Agua Viva*. Rio de Janeiro: Editora Artenova, 1973. *The Stream of Life*. Trans. Earl Fitz and Elizabeth Lowe. Minneapolis: University of Minnesota Press, 1989. p. 12.

Mikhalkov, Nikita. *Soleil trompeur* (*Burnt by the Sun*). Moscow/Paris: Studio Trite/Camera One, 1994. (Winner of Grand Prize, Cannes, 1994).

Pardis, Anna. "Conception." in Guillevic. p. 337.

Pelletier, Pol et. al. *La nef des sorcières*. Montreal: Quinze, 1976. *A Clash of Symbols*. Trans. Linda Gaboriau. Toronto: Coach House, 1979.

Proust, Marcel. *Du côté de chez Swann*. Paris: Gallimard, 1913. *Swann's Way*. Trans. C.K. Scott Moncrieff. London: Chatto and Windus, 1929.

Roubaud, Alix Cléo. *Journal 1979-1983*. Paris: Seuil, 1984.

Sartre, Jean-Paul. *L'Etre et le néant*. Paris: Gallimard, 1943. *Being and Nothingness*. Trans. Hazel E. Barnes. New York: Philosophical Library, 1956.

Schaffner, Perdita. "Pandora's Box." in H.D. *HERmione*. New York: New Directions, 1981. vii–xi. p. viii.

Sollers, Philippe. *Femmes*. Paris: Gallimard, 1983. *Women*. Trans. Barbara Bray. New York: Columbia University Press, 1990.

Wittgenstein, Ludwig. *Preliminary Studies for the Philosophical Investigations Generally Known as the Blue and Brown Books*. 2nd ed. Oxford: Basil Blackwell, 1958. p. 26.

Woolf, Virginia. *A Writer's Diary*. Ed. Leonard Woolf. London: Hogarth, 1953. *Journal d'un écrivain*. Trans. Germaine Beaumont. Paris: Union générale des éditeurs, 1977.

Yourcenar, Marguerite. "Comment Wang-Fô fut sauvé." in *Nouvelles orientales*. Paris: Gallimard, 1963. p. 9-34. "How Wang-Fô Was Saved." in *Oriental Tales*. Trans. Alberto Manguel. New York: Farrar Straus and Giroux, 1985.